KEYS TO
ESTATE PLANNING

Second Edition

D. Larry Crumbley, Ph.D., C.P.A.
Shelton Taxation Professor
Texas A&M University

Edward E. Milam, Ph.D., C.P.A.
Professor of Accounting
Mississippi State University

BARRON'S

All inquiries should be addressed to:
Barron's Educational Series, Inc.
250 Wireless Boulevard
Hauppauge, New York 11788

Library of Congress Catalog Card Number 93-22031

International Standard Book No. 0-8120-1710-2

Library of Congress Cataloging-in-Publication Data

Crumbley, D. Larry.
    Keys to estate planning and trusts / D. Larry Crumbley
and Edward E. Milam.—2nd ed.
      p.   cm.—(Barron's business keys)
    Rev. ed. of: Keys to estate planning. 1989.
    Includes index.
    ISBN 0-8120-1710-2
    1. Estate planning—United States.   2. Trusts and
trustees— United States.   I. Milam, Edward E.
II. Crumbley, D. Larry.   Keys to estate planning.
III. Title.   IV. Series.
KF750.C735   1993
346.7305'2—dc20
[347.30652]   93-22031
                                         CIP

PRINTED IN THE UNITED STATES OF AMERICA

456 9770 98765432

CONTENTS

INTRODUCTION

Everyone needs an estate plan. Whether a person is a business owner, an employee, or self-employed, whether of substantial wealth or of modest means, all of us should plan our estates. Estate planning includes building an estate during a lifetime, then seeing that those assets are protected in an estate that can be passed to the next generation. This book will help you gain basic knowledge of estate management. Although designed primarily for the novice, it may be used as a refresher for someone who has been away from estate planning for a time. After you have mastered each key, you will be better prepared to understand more specialized books and articles on estate planning and taxation.

The keys are designed so that you can go directly to any topic in which you may be interested. In addition, when a concept is used that is covered more fully elsewhere, the reader is referred to that key or keys. When a new word is introduced and explained, it will be printed in italics. This helps you move around within the book. The key format also allows you to read the book in short time segments, whenever you have a spare moment. On the other hand, it is also possible to read the book straight through from beginning to end.

Owing to the nature of the estate tax law, some references are made to the Internal Revenue Code. These references are indicated by the term "Section," followed by a number. For example, Section 72 refers to Section 72 of the Internal Revenue Code, referring to the taxability of annuity payments.

After reading this book, you should have a better idea of the many factors that must be carefully considered before drawing a will or making an estate plan. Competent, professional advice is, of course, essential. You need to know how to select and work with the estate planning team. The authors hope that the terms and concepts introduced here will help you understand more clearly the suggestions of your estate planning team, so that all of you, working together, can do a better job.

Remember: Review your estate plans frequently! Because so much of modern estate planning is tax motivated, reviews with your tax professional should be done, at the minimum, after the passage of any significant tax law change. Legislation has been introduced to reduce the estate tax credit from $192,800 to $54,800. Furthermore, President Clinton has indicated that he would consider taxing capital gains at a person's death. Either one of these changes would dramatically increase the impact of the estate tax. Estate management is a dynamic, ever-changing, living process that continues to have an effect after death.

1

ESTATE PLANNING IS IMPORTANT

Estate planning is the art of designing a program for the effective enjoyment, management, and disposition of property at the minimum possible tax cost. This process is much more than just planning for death. Estate planning tries to encourage a wealth-building approach for everyone. This process looks at the income tax, fiduciary tax, estate tax, and gift tax to minimize the overall tax burden of the total family unit. Building an estate throughout life should be part of estate planning. This book covers both the creation and conservation of an estate.

Anyone with income, property, and investments must be concerned with estate planning. It may be even more important to the owner of a medium-sized estate than to the owner of a large estate, because the waste of a single asset in such an estate could prevent the accomplishment of objectives and bring hardship to the family unit. In other words, everyone who owns assets needs an estate plan. The estate plan might be reflected by a simple *will* or by a complex arrangement consisting of several of the estate planning devices or tools available to the estate owner, such as a trust, charitable contributions, and life insurance. These and other factors will be explained in subsequent keys.

Before an estate plan becomes effective, the appropriate legal documents must be executed. The necessity for careful planning and execution of the legal documents cannot be overemphasized, for faulty execution is a sure way of altering or even invalidating any estate plan. Thus, these legal instruments must be drafted by a competent attorney who is well versed in estate planning techniques. Do not assume that any attorney can draft a will. A specialist in, say, real estate would not be conversant with the latest developments in estate work.

These documents should be reviewed periodically to ascertain that they continue to express the objectives of the estate owner. A periodic review of the financial status and family relationships should be conducted to determine if there have been any changes that necessitate a revision of the estate plan. For example, a divorce would necessitate a change in a person's will. Also, an estate plan should be reviewed in the light of any changes or potential changes in the relevant legal or tax aspects. Such a review could bring about a modification in the plan that would produce significant benefits to the estate owner, while the neglect of such a review could be very costly. Be aware that estate assets may escape tax in the first estate, only to be taxed at a higher rate in the surviving spouse's second estate.

Since death is uncertain, everyone, young or old, should be ready for the contingency of death at any time. Even with the great advances in modern medicine, not everyone is lucky enough to grow old gracefully.

2

ESTATE PLANNING TEAM

Many professional skills are useful in the estate planning process. Usually, a team effort works best. The attorney, the accountant (CPA), the trust officer, and the life insurance underwriter are the professionals most often associated with the team. In addition, there is now the growing profession of Certified Financial Planners.

The attorney's participation is most essential in determining the legal and tax consequences of every phase in the process of developing an estate plan. The lawyer must determine whether certain recommendations and phases in the formulation of the plan have legal substance and merit. Only a competent attorney can draft the legal documents that provide the framework for the execution of an effective estate plan. And only a lawyer can practice law legally.

Estate planning is the trust officer's prime concern not only because it is a device for developing new business, but also because it constitutes the bulk of the trust department's activities. The trust officer, who is essentially an instrument of estate conservation and management, can lend advice on the practicalities of the plan and play a major role in the administration of the estate. Under a specific agreement, he accepts custody of the property, manages and invests it, and distributes it to the beneficiaries according to the stipulations of the trust instrument. Just as an army travels on its stomach, estate planning often travels on the trust vehicle.

By virtue of their tendency toward salesmanship, life insurance underwriters may be the prime motivators in developing an estate plan that will eventually involve the orchestration of the other members of the estate planning team. An insurance agent whom you trust can often provide excellent advice and ideas, often uncovering situations where only a properly executed estate plan can save a taxpayer's estate from erosion. Also, the insurance underwriter has a specialized knowledge of the many forms of life insurance and knows what various policies can and cannot do.

Normally, the accountant (CPA) is considered to be the member of the estate planning team who is intimately acquainted with the financial affairs of the taxpayer and is knowledgeable about income and estate tax laws. In addition, the CPA is to advise on valuation problems and, in the case of a family business, to determine its existing and potential earning power. Otherwise, the accountant's role as a member of the estate planning team is not so easily ascertained or clearly defined as the roles of the other members; but because accountants know their client's affairs, they should recognize each client's need for estate planning services. Therefore, the accountant is often the person on the team who has the responsibility to initiate the estate process.

3

ESTATE ADMINISTRATION

Aside from the estate planning team, there are other players in the final estate administration. For example, the county or state probate court is an important participant. The functions of the probate court are to oversee the executor, conserve the decedent's assets, interpret the will, and, if there is no will, apply the laws of intestate succession. If someone dies without a will, this is called dying *intestate* (i.e., the state will write a will for you by statute).

The *will* designates an *executor* (man) or *executrix* (woman) to manage the assets and liabilities of the decedent—quite often the surviving spouse or a close relative. It is not an easy task and may be time-consuming. The job may last from nine months up to three years. The major roles of the executor are to search for all of the assets, publish notices to creditors in local newspapers, file appropriate estate and income tax returns, pay expenses and liabilities, and distribute the remaining assets to the beneficiaries of the estate. The executor will control only the *probate assets.* There are often assets in the *gross estate* that do not go through probate (i.e., jointly held property, life insurance proceeds, and trust assets). The American Bar Association estimates that executors' fees are approximately 5% of an estate.

The Internal Revenue Service is an obviously interested participant. The income tax return (Form 1040), the estate tax return (Form 706), and the estate income tax return (Form 1041) may be required. The taxation departments of the states and, in some instances, local governments have a greater or lesser role, depending on their statutory authority.

If a *trust* has been created during the lifetime of the decedent (called *inter vivos*) or at death (called *testamentary*), there will be a trustee named in the trust agreement to carry out the tax and nontax objectives of the trust. The trustee's responsibilities may last an entire generation. Either a corporate trustee, such as a banker, or nonprofessional trustee, such as a family member, may be chosen to carry out the fiduciary duties of this task. Or both types might be appointed to handle the job jointly.

4

WHY HAVE A WILL?

The will is a key vehicle of transfer at death, and its preparation is often the first step taken by people in planning the disposition of their estates. A will is a set of written instructions prepared under legal rules that directs how a person's property will be disposed of at death. Everybody needs a properly executed will, and a copy of the will should be kept *outside* the safe deposit box. If the only copy is inside, it may be impossible for the heirs or executors to get at it without a lot of time-consuming legal rigamarole.

Stories are legion about the disastrous consequences of dying intestate. In such a situation, the state laws direct how the assets will be distributed—a will by default. The county or state probate court will appoint an administrator, who may not be qualified to manage your estate. Most intestate succession laws favor the surviving spouse, child, or grandchildren. Assets, therefore, might go to children of a previous marriage, to distant nephews and nieces, or even to enemies. Furthermore, if there are no close relatives, your assets will go to the state. The estate process can drag on for many years. The lawyer(s) may get the bulk of the estate assets.

If you don't have a will, in effect you're allowing the state to draft a will for you after your death. And to decide who administers it! Most state laws assume that family members (and not friends) are the natural objects of one's bounty. Thus, for the nearly 2 million unmarried couples living together, dying without a will can have catastrophic consequences. Most state laws do not recognize a "living together" relationship. Certainly the law on intestate succession is especially problematic for homosexuals. (See Key 50).

Wills and estate plans are not once-in-a-lifetime documents. People outgrow their initial wills, and new laws make revision of wills essential. Also, amendments or revisions are necessary in case of marriage, divorce, birth of a child, death of a spouse or child, marriage of a child, increase or decrease in personal wealth, moving to a new state, purchase of life insurance, and more. Thus, estate planning is a lifelong process.

If a person runs a business, mention should be made in the will about operation of the business after his or her death. In some states an executor cannot lawfully continue a business without a specific authorization. The business operation may come to a halt, buildings may deteriorate, or the business may have to be liquidated if proper authority is not given. Thus, key issues in the will should cover valuation of the business, succession, or disposal.

The will is used to designate heirs, identify the property they are to receive, indicate the person (or institution) who will act as executor/executrix of the estate, and clarify similar details. Some useful provisions attached to the will are the *marital deduction* and the *marital deduction trusts.* The basic advantage of using the marital deduction is the favorable tax consequences. The cost of this tax savings, however, may be the compromise of the estate owner's objectives, the possible deferred increase in transfer costs, or the loss of control of an asset.

Married couples with small estates may wish to have a simple "I love you will." Here each spouse leaves all of his/her assets to the surviving spouse. Even in such cases, however, it is necessary that a legal arrangement be made for the assets to be left in a *trust* for any minor children in case both parties die simultaneously (such as in a plane accident). In legal terms, a *holographic* will is in one's own handwriting, and a *nuncupative* will is oral. An oral will is seldom valid.

Before a will is accepted for probate, the probate court determines whether the will is legal in substance and form. Generally, the testator (male) or testatrix (female) must sign the will in the presence of a specific number of witnesses. Two credible witnesses are necessary in most states (3 in South Carolina and Vermont). Credible refers to a competent person who can legally testify in a court.

The testator must not have been under undue influence and should be supervised by an authoritative party (i.e., an attorney). The will must be in a single document and must include an *attestation clause.* Such a clause is a single item before the testator's signature indicating that the testator signed the will in the presence of the appropriate number of witnesses *and* that the witnesses were present to witness the testator's signature. Be sure to destroy all of the draft copies of the final executed will.

A person may wish to specify in the will if they wish to be cremated or donate body parts to medical science for research. Anyone who is the parent or guardian of children under the age of 18 should appoint a guardian of the minor's property. Appointment of a guardian by will avoids the filing of a surety bond with the court. In essence, a will expresses the final wishes of the testator.

A *codicil* is an instrument that revokes, changes, or adds to the terms of a will. A *joint will* is one document that is signed by husband and wife. A *living* will is a separate document where a person expresses a wish that his or her life not be prolonged by artificial or extraordinary measures.

Briefly summarized in the following paragraphs are two other types of wills designed to provide adequately for surviving spouse and children, while paying as little in estate taxes as possible.

Assume that the husband dies first. In a two-part will, some assets pass directly to the surviving wife, with a minimum pecuniary amount specified (e.g., a will might state that no less than $300,000 is to go directly to the wife). She controls these assets. The remaining assets, up to the federal *exemption equivalent* (i.e., $600,000), go into a bypass trust, so that they are not taxed in the wife's estate either. If there are still assets left over beyond the exemption equivalent amount, they go directly to the wife (and qualify for the unlimited marital deduction).

In a three-part will, some assets go directly to the surviving wife, who controls them. Again, a minimum pecuniary amount may be specified. Also, as in the two-part will, some property goes directly to a bypass trust, up to the exemption equivalent. The remaining property passes to a *qualified terminable interest property* (QTIP) trust, with income to wife for life, and property going to children at wife's death. This is a very technical area, and a reader should discuss such a trust with a competent attorney (Key 45).

Of course, the kind of will that is best for a given person depends on the individual situation and may change as the person's circumstances change.

5

GATHERING THE FACTS

The facts themselves serve as the basis for designing and implementing an estate plan. Obtaining the facts may seem to be a simple task, but in many cases this is the most challenging part of the estate planning process. The facts needed can be classified into four categories: domicile, property, beneficiaries, and the individual's objectives.

Domicile refers to the permanent home of a person and is important because it determines the law that will govern the validity of the will and its provision. Domicile determines how title to property is held: *community property* versus *separate* property and *joint tenancy* versus a *tenancy in common.* Because the differences that exist between real property laws of differing states are significant, the domicile of the estate owner must be determined before plans are formulated. All indicia of domicile should point to one state (auto registration, voter registration, will provisions, where income taxes are filed, etc.). Otherwise, different states will try to tax your assets.

A complete inventory of a taxpayer's property—assets minus liabilities—should be gathered. Such data would include *insurance* policies, *powers of appointment,* property owned separately and jointly, business interests, retirement and death benefits, claims under wills and trusts, and rights in *future interests.* In addition to these data, full information about the estate owner's obligations must be secured. These details include information about personal debts, business debts, accrued taxes, mortgages, leases, installment contracts, and all other debts, including contingent liabilities.

Special problems concerning an estate owner's business interests often arise in the analysis of his/her property, especially when these interests amount to a large portion of the estate. Business ownership causes a problem of valuation. These interests must be properly valued for estate tax purposes in accordance with the Internal Revenue Code and Regulations. (See also Revenue Ruling 59-60, which can be found in the 1959 *Cumulative Bulletin.*) Another problem is the determination and the ability of the business to produce income for the benefit of the taxpayer's heirs after his/her death or retirement. Even when a business is the chief source of its owner's income and wealth and will continue to be so as long as it is actively managed by the owner, it may not continue to be profitable after the owner leaves or dies.

Facts concerning the beneficiaries of the estate owner must be gathered and accumulated by the estate owner or the estate planning team. These facts should include the names and birthdates of the estate owner and all of his/her beneficiaries. An evaluation should be made of the estate owner's responsibility to the family. Such personal information as the character of the estate owner's spouse and other heirs and their business abilities should be considered. A taxpayer's state of health, the wealth now available to the heirs, their financial needs, and the attitudes of individual beneficiaries toward each other are important. In summary, estate owners should obtain data about the health, wealth, education, character, and living needs of all their beneficiaries.

Finally, the objectives of the estate owner must be formulated. Many people feel that their heirs should have complete and unrestricted freedom to use the assets left to them, while others have a fear of entrusting substantial amounts of money in lump sums to their beneficiaries. Family and human considerations may take precedence over tax considerations. For example, one of the authors heard a business owner state his estate objectives as follows: "I have told my children that if there is one thin dime left when I die, then that was a mistake on my part." Although few people will have such an attitude, making a determination of an estate owner's objectives is critical in the development of an estate plan. It is very often the most difficult phase of gathering the facts.

In addition to gathering the facts, an estate owner must determine and evaluate his/her existing estate plan. Whether estate owners are aware of it or not, they have an estate plan that may have been developed consciously or accidentally. Therefore, people must accumulate information concerning all gifts, trusts, wills, and reversionary interests they create or possess. Many estate owners who have not made such a thorough analysis of their estates have been surprised at the results. Such an analysis is necessary to lay a firm foundation for the remainder of the estate planning process.

6

SELECTING AN ATTORNEY

How do I find a good lawyer to prepare a will? Any search for an effective estate planning attorney involves methods of locating qualified attorneys as well as the ideal qualities to look for in an attorney.

Various methods exist for locating an estate planning attorney. Those attorneys who are certified in the estate planning field will advertise this fact. A city or county estate planning council will provide an individual with the names of various attorneys. Another worthwhile source is the opinions of several trust officers in regard to the most competent attorneys in their field. Business associates and friends can provide the names of attorneys whom they feel comfortable enough to recommend.

Go to a local library and locate *The Bar Register,* which is published annually with those lawyers who enjoy fine professional reputations. Also, the *Martindale-Hubbell Law Directory* lists every attorney in the United States, rating their legal ability.

The proper level of competence required of a lawyer is dependent on the nature and extent of your wealth. Most smaller estates only require a simple will, which can be handled by any general practitioner. But where estate taxes might be incurred, or where there are any unusual circumstances, such as a child who is not competent to manage his/her own affairs, it is best to find an attorney who specializes in estate planning and administration.

Two important attributes for an attorney in this field are sensitivity and compassion. The best attorney is one who adopts the attitude of a counselor and takes the time and effort to be extremely conscious of your needs, hopes, and fears and those of your beneficiaries.

Choosing an attorney who can communicate effectively is essential. This attribute includes communicating not only with you, but also with other professionals on the estate planning team.

Last but certainly not least, you must pick an attorney that you can afford. Demand written knowledge of your attorney's hourly fee and an estimate of the cost of preparing your will and planning your estate before he/she begins work. Shop around. Lawyers can be expensive, but the costs of estate planning can be offset by the conservation of the total estate. Finding the best advisor who will do a good job at a reasonable cost does take patience.

The American Bar Association estimates that attorneys' fees are approximately 6½% of an estate. In addition, filing fees may be as high as $1,000 in some areas.

7

TITLE TO PROPERTY

Property can be owned several major ways: fee simple, tenancy in common, joint tenancy with rights of survivorship, and community property.

Fee simple ownership means outright ownership by yourself alone. A fee simple owner is a sole and absolute owner. Fee simple property is included in the gross estate at fair market value on date of death.

There are various types of joint ownership of property. A *tenancy in common* is an undivided interest that can be transferred during life or death. In other words, to own property in tenancy in common is to own it with one or more other people. For example, you may own a duplex with another person. Each of you own half of the duplex. You can sell your half during your lifetime. At death, the applicable portion of the undivided interest is included in gross estate (i.e., one-half of the duplex).

As for *joint tenancy with rights of survivorship,* you own all of the property with someone else. You can give your interest away, or you can sell it. But you cannot leave your interest to anyone at death because the property automatically passes to the surviving tenant.

The tax rules for property held jointly by spouses with survivorship rights are fairly simple. Each spouse is to be treated as one-half owner of joint tenancy assets, regardless of which spouse furnished the funds to acquire the property and regardless of how the joint tenancy was created. Thus, the first spouse to die includes one-half of the joint tenancy in gross estate, and only one-half of any separate property will receive a step-up in basis. (Step-up in basis is the difference between the price the decedent originally paid for an asset and its fair market value when an heir receives it.) If an asset's value has increased, the resulting gain to the heir is not taxable to the heir, either when he/she receives the asset or when he/she eventually disposes of it. This is an extremely important concept in tax planning.

For example, a married couple owns a $190,000 house (that cost them $40,000 many years ago) in a separate-property state. Husband dies in 1993, and one-half of the value of the house is included in his gross estate, but it is not taxed because of the unlimited marital deduction. Wife receives the home under the will with a basis of $115,000 ($20,000 + $95,000).

Assume that in this example the husband owns the house outright and dies first. Husband could leave the house to wife and obtain a marital deduction for the will transfer, paying no estate taxes. Here the wife would receive a full step-up in basis to $190,000.

If the wife in the first example sells the home, she would have a $75,000 potential taxable gain, but the wife in the second example would have none. As these two examples demonstrate, joint ownership of property by married couples may no longer be appropriate because of the unlimited marital deduction. However, with the current high divorce rate, who is to own the property: husband or wife?

There are two types of states: common law states and community property states. The nine community property law states are Arizona, California, Idaho, Louisiana, Nevada, New Mexico, Texas, Washington, and Wisconsin. All other states are classified as common law states.

This concept of community property came from France and Spain. A person's domicile determines the type of property at the time the property is acquired. In general, only property acquired during a marriage is community property. In community property states, any property acquired by spouses during marriage is construed to be one total community of property (i.e., they are 50-50 partners).

For tax purposes, only one-half of the community property is included in the gross estate. Jointly held property in a community-property state will include a full step-up in basis, including the surviving spouse's one-half interest in the community property. Thus, joint ownership in a community-property state in order to avoid probate is still satisfactory.

For example, Bill Blair owns his home in Texas (a community-property state) jointly with rights of survivorship with his wife, Mary. Bill paid $70,000 for their home. At the death of Bill in 1993, the house is valued at $230,000. Mary later sells the house for $240,000 and remarries. Mary would receive a full step-up in basis to $230,000, which is not taxable. However, the $10,000 difference between market value at Bill's death and the price she eventually receives for the house would be considered potential taxable gain.

8

THE PROBATE PROCESS

The probate system normally starts with a petition to a state court explaining who died and when. Accordingly, probate is a legal process. The petition describes the estate assets and asks the state court to accept the will as authentic. If there is no will (i.e., someone who has died intestate), then the court will "write" a will based upon state statutes. Notices will be mailed to all parties mentioned in the will and to all legal relatives, as defined by the state law.

The probate process is intended to protect the relations of the decedent by ascertaining the authenticity of the will, notifying creditors to present claims against the estate, and appointing an executor to carry out the details of the probate process.

After the notice process is complete, the state court sets a date to admit the will to probate. Any person with an interest in the estate can object, including the court itself. For example, if a spouse or potential heir is omitted from the will, that person may object. These objections are made public.

Before a will is accepted for probate, the probate court determines whether the will is legal in both substance and form. If there are no objections in the state court, the court will then admit the will to probate and issue a letter of testamentary. This letter appoints the entity or person named in the will as the executor or executrix. The executor now has the power to distribute the assets to the appropriate heirs. Once all distributions have been made, releases are given to the executor and the estate is closed.

Be aware that this simple process may take up to

five years to complete. If the decedent has property in more than one state, there will be ancillary probates in those other states where such property is located.

As a result of the high costs and length of probate, some people try to avoid probate entirely. Key 9 discusses ways to avoid probate. It should help you decide whether or not you even wish to avoid probate.

9

AVOIDING PROBATE

All property subject to probate or to court disposition becomes public record and thus is open to public scrutiny. The sure way to avoid these public disclosures and the inevitable legal and other expenses associated with this process is to avoid probate.

In a smaller estate, probate can be avoided by holding property jointly between spouses. On the death of the first spouse, all of the property goes to the surviving spouse outside of probate. Administration expenses are thus reduced. Such jointly held property may be exempt from state inheritance taxes along with disclosure and reporting requirements.

However, these assets may be lost to the creditors or to the spouse of your joint owner. For example, two brothers are joint tenants in a business building that is leased to someone else. Since they are tenants in common, creditors of either brother can get 50% of the building. If one brother dies, his heirs will inherit 50% of the building and may force the surviving brother to sell the remaining asset.

Estate owners also can avoid probate by placing their properties in a revocable trust for the benefit of their survivors (so-called living trust). The trust becomes irrevocable upon the grantor's death. The fact is that property left in trust is not subject to probate and does not become part of the basis from which the executor's and attorney's fees are determined. Thus, by placing the property in trust, the estate owner avoids the public scrutiny and reduces the amount of the executor's fees that this estate would have to pay. Also, disgruntled relatives are more prone to attack the capacity of estate owners to make a will than the right of the estate owner to establish an *inter vivos* trust.

Lifetime giving is another way to avoid probate (see Keys 28–33). Another important point is that life insurance proceeds paid to a named beneficiary are not subject to probate.

You avoid probate on life insurance by designating a beneficiary and contingent beneficiary when you purchase the insurance. They will automatically receive the insurance proceeds on your death. It is wise to add the words, "per stirpes" after the name of the beneficiary (i.e., "to my wife per stirpes"). These Latin words mean to leave the proceeds to the named beneficiary, or—if he or she should predecease you—to the heirs.

Several other types of assets avoid probate by your naming the beneficiary on the ownership papers:

1. Disability insurance policies.
2. Annuities.
3. Individual retirement accounts.
4. Pension plans such as Section 401(k), Keogh, and profit-sharing plans.

Be careful about designating your children as the receivers of an individual retirement account because they cannot get the favorable tax treatment that your spouse can.

A custodial account under the Uniform Gifts to Minors Act may be established for a minor in order to avoid probate. An irrevocable gift is made to the minor, with a custodian appointed to manage the funds. If the grantor is named the custodian, the funds may be subject to estate tax upon the death of the grantor. Under this circumstance, these non-probate assets are still part of the decedent's taxable estate and may be taxed (Key 12). Thus, the cost of avoiding probate is paid by you during your life in the form of attorney or trustee fees with little, if any, reduction in federal estate taxes upon your death.

A revocable living trust may be appropriate in these situations:

1. You desire privacy.
2. Your estate is large or complex.
3. You own real estate in more than one state.
4. Your state has a cumbersome or expensive probate process.
5. Your will may be contested.
6. You wish to keep a portion of your assets separate.

Finally, the Uniform Probate Code allows for a simplified process which gives the protection of a court procedure without as much expense.

(For more details about avoiding probate, see A.G. Berg, *Keys to Avoiding Probate and Reducing Estate Taxes*, 1992, Barron's.)

10

POWERS OF ATTORNEY

A power of attorney is a legal document whereby a person gives the right to handle all or part of his or her assets to another person. In effect, the other person is your substitute in case you are unable to act for yourself with respect to a legal, financial, or real estate matter. This technique is especially appropriate for younger people in special circumstances (e.g., out of the country for a period of time) and elderly individuals. According to estimates, 25% of the U.S. population will be over the age of 65 by the year 2000.

A person or institution may have your power of attorney to do almost anything, from signing one check to running your small business. There are several types of powers of attorney:

1. General power of attorney.
2. Specific power of attorney.
3. Durable power of attorney.
4. Springing power of attorney.

The general power of attorney may be the trickiest. In this instance, the principal nominates another person (the agent or attorney-in-fact) to act on the principal's behalf. Many times, the spouse is named as the attorney-in-fact. Often, there may be more than one agent (e.g., spouse and a child), so the formal document should clearly state whether the named agents are authorized to act separately or must act jointly. This traditional power of attorney can be revoked at any time while the principal is competent. The document terminates on your death or when you become incompetent.

A specific power of attorney gives only a limited power, as outlined in the document. For example, a taxpayer can grant a specific power of attorney to the IRS by using IRS Form 2848 or Form 2848D. The latter gives less authority to the designated person, so Form 2848D should be considered whenever possible. A power of attorney may be granted without using Form 2848, but all information that would normally be provided on the IRS form must be given. An unenrolled representative who does not file the form may be prohibited from receiving or inspecting certain tax information.

To be considered valid, a tax power of attorney must contain certain information about you. This includes your name, identification number, and address. If a joint return is being filed and both spouses are naming the same representative, the identical information must be provided for the spouse. Your representative's name, Central Authorization File (CAF) number (if already assigned), address, and telephone number must be designated. The IRS assigns the CAF number after your representative files a Form 2848 or Form 2848D with an IRS office.

A durable power of attorney allows the power to remain in effect after the principal becomes incompetent. Durable powers permit individuals to avoid guardianship by establishing non-court regimes for the management of their affairs in the event of later incompetency. Think of it as senility insurance comparable to that available to relatively wealthy people who use funded revocable trusts for the same purpose.

Most states including the District of Columbia recognize a durable power of attorney. Generally, the document should contain a durability clause such as follows:

This power of attorney shall not be affected by the subsequent disability or incompetence of the principal.

The principal's signature should be witnessed or acknowledged by a notary public. A durability clause will allow a person to avoid a court proceeding in the event of Alzheimer's disease or some other incapacitating illness.

About 20 states, including New York, California, and Michigan, recognize a special type of durable power of attorney called a springing power of attorney. The power of attorney "springs" into effect when a specified event occurs. These springing powers allow a person to maintain control over his or her affairs as long as possible. For example, the general or specific power of attorney remains dormant unless you become physically or mentally incompetent, or you enter a nursing home.

In states not recognizing springing powers, similar results can be achieved. Have your attorney draft a document with the executed power together with a letter specifying that the power of attorney is to be released upon the occurrence of certain events.

11

WEALTH TRANSFER

In these days of inflation, investments grow in value more rapidly than ever before. Many people are surprised that they have problems with a tax that they have never heard of before: the estate tax. The federal government imposes a tax on the *fair market value* of all taxable assets, less liabilities, held by a person at death. This amount includes the home, all life insurance (even though paid to someone else), and property owned jointly with someone else. The first $600,000 of a person's estate who dies is not taxable ($1,200,000 in a community property state). The law is written so that the first $192,800 of estate taxes is not paid, which converts into a taxable estate of about $600,000. Thereafter, the tax graduates from 32% up to an eventual 55% in the highest bracket for taxable estates over $3 million.

Many state governments also impose inheritance taxes on the amounts received by the individual heirs. Here again there is usually an exemption for a certain amount of property, depending upon the relationship of the heir to the person who died. However, there are many instances where the federal and state death taxes consumed a major portion of the decedent's estate where there was inadequate tax planning. For example, the late Howard Hunt left an estate of about $460 million. The death taxes on his estate were 77% because he died in 1976 without a will!

Gift taxes and estate taxes are excise taxes imposed on the transfer of a taxable amount of property during the life or upon death. They are also called succession taxes and transfer taxes. On transfers during life the primary liability for payment of any resulting gift tax is on the donor. If he or she does not pay it, the donee has secondary liability. The estate tax is imposed on the aggregate value of all property left by a decedent after reduction by deductions and credits, and is payable by the estate's executor or administrator out of that property. The degree of kinship, if any, of heirs to the decedent is immaterial.

An estate tax differs from an inheritance tax. The latter is imposed by most states and is based on the value of property passing to each particular heir. The exempt amounts and tax rates depend upon the degree of kinship of the heir to the decedent and the value of the property passing to the particular heir. The primary liability for payment is on the heir, but decedents' wills frequently provide for payment of state inheritance taxes out of the residuary estate. A few states also have an estate tax. Less than a handful impose a gift tax.

12

GROSS ESTATE

Before any estimate can project the amount of estate tax to be paid on the death of an individual, one must know what assets are included in the gross estate and also the value to be placed on them. Without knowledge of these two things, the estate planner is helpless in estimating the potential estate tax. All the property, including real or personal, tangible or intangible, owned in whole or in part by the decedent at the time of death is included in gross estate to the extent of the value of any interest in such property. This includes any real property located outside the United States. Since the gross estate includes the value of the decedent's interest in all property owned at his death, ownership is an important factor in determining the gross estate. Normally, local property law controls the issue of ownership for tax purposes. In some circumstances this is a highly complex matter.

A decedent's gross estate is composed of a wide variety of "owned" property. The gross estate also includes certain other assets in which the interest of the decedent is considered to be substantially equivalent to ownership even though the decedent held no legal interest in the property at the time of death. In other words, the decedent still has some "strings" attached to the property.

A *remainder interest* or other *future interest* in property is pulled into gross estate by Section 2033 of the U. S. Internal Revenue Code, unless the interest is a *contingent remainder* or some other future interest that terminates upon the death of a decedent. A *contingent remainder* is an interest that does not come into enjoyment and possession unless a certain condition or contingency occurs or an interest that may terminate upon the occurrence (or nonoccurrence) of an event in the future. The death of an individual without children or before a specific date are examples of such an event.

As a general rule, when a person retains an interest in a transferred property, but that interest is contingent on the person remaining alive, Section 2033 does not pull such an interest into gross estate.

A *vested remainder* is pulled into the estate of a remainder person who dies before obtaining such property interest. However, a remainder interest is limited to the remainder person's life since his interest in the property interest terminates at his death.

An example is helpful. Suppose Don transfers assets to a trust with income to his wife, Ann, for life, with remainder to his son, Bob (if living), and any remainder to his nephew, Carl (or Carl's estate). If Bob dies but is survived by Ann, nothing will be included in Bob's estate since the interest evaporates at his death. Carl's interest became vested upon Bob's death. If Carl dies, survived by Ann but not Bob, Carl's interest is included in his estate. Obviously, for tax-planning purposes it is advantageous to give a person a remainder that is dependent upon his/her survival (that is, "if living") rather than an absolute interest (that is, "or to his/her estate").

The gross estate of a decedent includes the value of all property passing to the surviving spouse as dower or curtesy or by virtue of a statute creating an estate in lieu of dower and curtesy as determined by the laws of the specific state. A *dower* (to the wife) or *curtesy* (to the husband) is a statutory provision in a common-law state that directs a certain portion of the estate to the surviving spouse (often one third of the estate). However, state law does not determine the tax status of that interest under the federal statute.

For example, suppose wife without a will is killed in a car accident, leaving an estate of $900,000. Under the state law, husband is entitled to one third of the wife's estate. The $300,000 that the husband receives is included in the wife's gross estate under Section 2034.

The gross estate also includes *retained life estates* and *transfers taking effect at death,* as explained in the next several keys. See also Key 31 for an explanation of lifetime gifts to remove property from an estate.

13

RETAINED LIFE INTEREST

Some incomplete gifts will be included in the gross estate. Incomplete gifts may include a retained life estate. A transfer with a retained life interest is included in the gross estate. Included under this concept is the value of all property or property interest transferred by a decedent, by trust or otherwise, if the decedent retained it for life or for another period defined by law. Specifically, under the federal statute, such interest is identified by

1. The possession, right to income, or other enjoyment of the property [Section 2036 (a) (1)].
2. The right, either alone or in conjunction with any other person, to designate who shall possess or enjoy the property or the income therefrom [Section 2036(a)(2)].

According to regulations, the use, possession, right to the income, or other enjoyment of the property is considered as having been retained by the decedent if it is to be applied to the discharge of any of his/her legal obligations, including the obligation during his/her lifetime to support a dependent. The phrase "right . . . to designate the person or persons who shall possess or enjoy the transferred property or the income therefrom" does not apply to a power held solely by a person other than the decedent. But if the decedent reserved the unrestricted power to remove a trustee at any time and appoint himself/herself as trustee, the decedent is considered as having the powers of the trustee.

Suppose a husband created a trust naming an independent party the trustee. Any income from this trust was to go to his three minor children to be used to help satisfy his obligation to support them. After the children reached age 18, the income interests were to continue for each of their lives. At the death of each child, one third of the trust was to pass to each child's children. Husband died when his children were 12, 15, and 23 years of age. Since two thirds of the trust income was being used to satisfy the legal obligation of support, two thirds of the trust assets would be included in husband's gross estate under Section 2036.

Retaining the right to vote, either directly or indirectly, on shares of stock of a controlled corporation is considered to be a retention of the enjoyment of the stock for purposes of Section 2036(a). Control refers to the ownership of, or the right to vote, in stock possessing at least 20% of the total combined voting power of all classes of stock. The transfer of nonvoting shares would not seem to fall within Section 2036(b), even where the decedent retained shares with voting rights.

A relinquishment or cessation of voting rights is treated as a *gift in contemplation of death* under Section 2035 (see Key 30). However, this is a problem only if the corporation was a controlled one at some time after the transfer and within three years of death.

14

DEATH TRANSFERS

Transfers taking effect at death must be included in the gross estate under Section 2037. The decedent's gross estate must include the value of any interest in property transferred by the decedent in any way, except for an adequate and full consideration in money or money's worth, if all the following conditions are met:

1. Possession or enjoyment of the property could, through ownership of the interest, have been obtained only by surviving the decedent.

2. The decedent has retained a reversionary interest in the transferred property by the expressed terms of the instrument of transfer.

3. The value of the reversionary interest immediately before the death of the decedent exceeds 5% of the value of the transferred property.

For purposes of this section, the term reversionary interest includes the possibility that property transferred by the decedent may return to the decedent or his estate or may be subject to a power of disposition by the decedent. This term does not include rights to income only. The value of such reversionary interest is determined by the usual methods of valuation, including the use of mortality tables and actuarial principles. In essence, whereas a transfer with a retained life estate (Section 2036) pulls in the entire amount of the property, a transfer taking effect at death (Section 2037) pulls in *some* of the property.

Suppose an individual (decedent) transfers property to a trust with the income payable to his wife for life and with the remainder payable to the decedent or, if he is not living at his wife's death, to his daughter or her estate. The daughter could not obtain possession or enjoyment of the property without surviving the decedent. Assume the decedent's reversionary interest immediately before his death exceeded 5% of the value of the property. The value of the property, less the value of the wife's outstanding life estate, is includable in the decedent's gross estate under Section 2037.

As an example, the transfer of property to a so-called *Clifford trust* is a retention of a reversionary interest. If the grantor dies before the termination of a Clifford trust, Section 2037 pulls the trust assets into the grantor's taxable estate. Also, a Totten trust could create the same result if the minor dies before reaching majority. In this area, one or more of these transfer sections may be used by the IRS in tandem in order to "reel in" an incomplete transfer.

15

REVOCABLE TRANSFERS

Property transferred during the decedent's lifetime is includable in the decedent's gross estate if at the time of death the enjoyment of the property was subject to change through the exercise of a power to alter, amend, revoke, or terminate by the decedent, either alone or in conjunction with another person.

A revocable trust does not have any income or estate tax advantages. In essence, the one who created the trust (called the grantor) may revoke the trust, often merely by sending a written notice to the trustee. A revocable trust might be useful under certain circumstances, such as an extended trip taken by the grantor where he or she might be out of touch for long periods of time, thus be unable to deal with any emergencies or other matters that came up concerning the property.

According to regulations, this provision does not apply (1) to the extent that the transfer was for adequate and full consideration in money or money's worth, or (2) if the decedent's power could be exercised only with the consent of all parties having an interest in the transferred property, or (3) to a power held solely by a person other than the decedent.

The regulations provide actuarial tables that must be used for determining life estates, annuities, terms for years, remainders, and reversions. Conditions other than the tables may be considered only if the individual is known to have been afflicted at the time of the transfer with an incurable physical condition that is in such an advanced stage that death is clearly imminent. There is a rebuttable presumption in favor of the use of these tables. This becomes an issue most often in the sale of an annuity.

Revocable living trusts have become popular as a means of avoiding probate (Key 9). However, the basic revocable living trust does not reduce federal estate taxes.

16

ANNUITIES

The gross estate includes the value of an annuity or other payment receivable by a beneficiary by reason of surviving the decedent under any form of contract or agreement, including employment plans and agreements (except life insurance contracts), when the value of the annuity or other payment is attributable to contributions made by the decedent or his/her employer. This inclusion is true if (1) the payment or annuity was payable to the decedent or (2) the decedent possessed the right to receive such annuity or payment, either alone or in conjunction with another, for his/her life or for any period not ascertainable without reference to death or for any period that does not in fact end before his/her death.

The amount included in the gross estate under such a contract is limited to the part of the value of the annuity receivable that is proportionate to the part of the purchase price contributed by the decedent or the decedent's employer. For this purpose, any contribution made by the decedent's employer or former employer as a consequence of employment is considered as being contributed by the decedent. There is excluded, however, the value of annuities or other benefits receivable by a beneficiary (other than the estate) under certain qualified employee benefit plans. This exclusion applies only to the benefits attributable to the employer's contributions. Further, an annuity that terminates at the decedent's death (that is, a single-life, nonrefund annuity) is not included in the decedent's gross estate.

Private annuities represent another important vehicle of transfer. However, careful consideration must be given to the risks involved. In such a contract, the annuitant transfers property other than cash to the obligor in return for the obligor's unsecured promise to make periodic payments of money to the annuitant for a specific period of time. The period of time is usually for the life of the annuitant. Thus, the major risk to the annuitant is the obligor's failure to make the required payments.

Fortunately, the private annuity offers several tax advantages. First, since this is a valid sales contract, the property is removed from the estate of the obligor. Second, Section 72 of the Internal Revenue Code governs the income taxability of the annuity payments. Thus, each annuity payment is broken into three portions: an excluded portion, an ordinary income portion, and a capital gain or loss portion. This gives the annuitant the additional advantage of spreading any gain from the sale of such property over a period of several years for income tax purposes. In essence, it gives the annuitant a deferment for payment of income taxes associated with the transfer.

An offshoot to the private annuity is an annuity structured so that the transferee's obligation to make periodic payments ends at the earlier of a fixed term of years (which must equal or exceed the transferor's actuarial life expectancy), or the death of the transferor. Called a PATY, the fair market value of the remaining contractual payments to be made to the transferee are not included in gross estate. As long as the fair market value of the property transferred is the same as the present value of the annuity received, there will be no taxable gift to the transferor or transferee. A PATY may be used to maximize payments to an ill relative without a gift tax, while minimizing the transferor's (or estate's) taxable gain.

17

GRANTING POWERS OF APPOINTMENT

The value of all property over which a decedent possessed a *general power of appointment* at the time of death is includable in gross estate. A general power of appointment is one under which holders have the right to dispose of the property in favor of (1) themselves, (2) their estate, (3) their creditors, or (4) the creditors of their estate. In essence, if one should exercise a general power of appointment during lifetime, there is a taxable gift. But if the general power is held at death, the property is included in the gross estate under Section 2041.

There are some exceptions to this definition of a general power of appointment:

1. When the holder's right to consume or invade the property is limited by an ascertainable standard relating to his/her needs for health, maintenance, support, or education, the power is not considered to be a general power of appointment.
2. If the power was created on or before October 21, 1942, and is exercisable by the decedent only in conjunction with another person, it is not general.
3. If the power was created after October 21, 1942, and is exercisable by the decedent only in conjunction with the creator of the power or with a person having substantial interest in the proper-

ty subject to the power in the decedent's favor, it is excluded.

4. If the power may be exercised both in favor of the decedent and the persons whose consent the decedent must have, the power is general to the extent of the decedent's fractional interest in it.

A general power is different from a *special* power of appointment. A special power of appointment may appoint anyone other than the four parties mentioned above. An individual may hold a special power of appointment at death and not include the property in the gross estate.

People who have a general power of appointment are treated for estate and gift tax purposes as if they own the property. If they exercise the general power during their lifetime, they pay a gift tax. If they hold onto the power (die without exercising it), the property is included in their gross estate. As a general rule, one should not give a general power of appointment.

Assume that Mr. Devine gives property to a trust, giving his grandson income for life, with a power to appoint to anyone except himself, his estate, his creditors, or his estate's creditors. The grandson could be given the power "to invade corpus in order to survive, to maintain himself, or to support himself." By giving the grandson a *special* power of appointment, the grandson could defer the generation-skipping tax by exercising the special power to create a present interest in a beneficiary in the same generation as the grandson (such as the grandson's spouse). If a grandson had been given a general power of appointment, there would be a tax at the time of the grandson's death.

The estate planning could go a step further. The grandson could be given the noncumulative power to invade corpus on December 31 of each year to the extent of $5,000 or 5% of the corpus (whichever is greater). This is called a Crummey power (which is a general power of appointment only on December 31).

Important, however, is that the gift is a present interest and qualifies for the annual exclusion. A lapse of a general power of appointment triggers estate and gift tax consequences. But a lapse is not treated as a release (i.e., taxable) unless the power exceeds in value, at the time of the lapse, the greater of $5,000 or 5% of the property. Therefore, this contingency distribution would not be included in the taxable estate or gift. To avoid income tax problems the beneficiary should be given about one month to disclaim the power.

Often, in a *marital trust,* the trustees have the discretionary power to invade principal in favor of the surviving spouse's well-being, maintenance, and health (that is, an ascertainable standard). Where the marital trust and the residuary trust are quite wealthy, it may be advisable to provide the surviving spouse with enough flexibility to invade the corpus of the marital trust in order to allow lifetime gifts to other family members. Remember that the principal of the marital trust is included in the surviving spouse's estate because of his/her testamentary power of appointment; thus, reduction of the value of the trust's principal through lifetime gifts may be wise.

18

VALUATION OF AN ESTATE

The value of assets for estate and gift tax purposes is at fair market value. This is the price between a willing buyer and willing seller, each with disclosure of material facts, and not under compulsion to sell. This fair market value is never determined by a forced sale price or by the sale of the item in a market other than that in which the item is most commonly sold. Therefore, if a particular item of property is normally retailed, the fair market value of the item to be included in the decedent's gross estate (or gross gift) is the price at which the item or a comparable item would be sold at retail.

For example, an automobile is generally retailed; thus, its fair market value would be the price at which a similar automobile could be purchased by a member of the general public, not by a dealer in used cars. The selling price of tangible personal property sold at a public auction or through newspaper classified advertising is deemed the retail price for estate tax purposes. To qualify, the sale must be made within a reasonable period following the applicable valuation date, when there is no substantial change in market conditions or other circumstances affecting the value of similar items between the time of sale and the applicable valuation date. Further, for estate tax purposes, property shall not be valued at the basis at which it is assessed for local tax purposes unless that assessed value represents the fair market value on the applicable valuation date.

Stocks and bonds are included in the decedent's gross estate at their fair market value per share or per bond on the valuation date. This fair market value is the mean value between the highest and lowest selling prices on the date of valuation. When there are sales on dates within a reasonable period of time both before and after the valuation date but no sale on the valuation date, the fair market value is the weighted average of the means between the highest and lowest sales on the nearest dates both before and after the valuation date. This average should be weighted inversely by the respective numbers of trading days between the valuation date and the nearest selling date. If there are no actual sales within a reasonable period of time of the valuation date, then the fair market value is considered to be the mean between the bona fide bid-and-asked prices on the date of valuation.

If it can be established that the value of stocks and bonds, determined on the basis of selling prices or on bid-and-asked prices, does not reflect the fair market value, then other relevant facts and elements must be considered in determining the fair market value. For example, if a block of stock is so large in relation to actual sales on the existing market that it could not be liquidated in a reasonable time without depressing the market, or if the block represents a controlling interest, then the price at which other lots change hands may have little relation to the true market value.

The fair market value of a decedent's interest in any business is the net amount that a willing buyer would pay a willing seller for such interest, neither being under any compulsion to buy or to sell, and both having reasonable knowledge of all the facts. A fair appraisal should be made of the earning capacity of the business and of all its assets, including goodwill. These elements should be considered in determining its net value. However, the value of a business interest may be fixed by a mutual buy-and-sell agreement. For such an agreement to be effective for estate tax purposes, it must bind the estate to sell, either by giving the survivors an option or by binding all parties, and the price must not be so grossly inadequate as to make the agreement a "mere gratuitous promise."

Generally, the fair market value of the decedent's household and personal effects is considered to be the price that a willing buyer would pay to a willing seller. There should be a room-by-room itemization of these articles. A separate value should be listed for each item; however, all articles in a room worth $100 or less may be grouped together. Instead of making such an itemized list, the executor may submit a written statement containing the aggregate value of the property as appraised by a competent appraiser. But if there are included among these household and personal effects any articles having a value of more than $3,000, the appraisal of an expert must be filed with the estate tax return. Before the executor may sell or distribute any of the household or personal effects in advance of an investigation by an officer of the IRS, he must give the district director notice of such action. This notice must be accompanied by an appraisal of such property.

Real property is to be valued under Reg. 20.2031-1 at its "highest and best use." This phrase means the most profitable use to which the property might logically and probably be put. The one exception is the *special-use valuation* method under Section 2032A.

The fair market value of annuities, life estates, terms for years, remainders, and reversions is their present value. The regulations provide tables to be used in calculating the present value of these assets. The value of a contract for the payment of an annuity or an insurance policy on the life of another person is the price for which such a contract could be acquired on the date of the decedent's death from a company regularly engaged in selling contracts of that character. If further premiums are to be paid on a life insurance policy on the life of another person, the value of such a policy may be approximated by adding to the interpolated terminal reserve at the date of the decedent's death the proportionate part of the gross premium that was last paid before the decedent's death and that covers the period extending beyond that date.

19

ALTERNATE VALUATION DATE

Although all property belonging to the decedent on the date of death is included in the gross estate and is generally appraised at its fair market value, the executor may elect to value the estate either at the date of the decedent's death or as of the date six months (not 180 days) after the decedent's date of death. This latter date is referred to as the alternate valuation date (AVD). Your will may remind your executor to consider the AVD.

If the alternate valuation date is to be used, the executor must make such an election on the estate tax return. In no case may such an election be made or a previous election be changed after the date of the tax return. When the AVD is elected, it applies to all property of the gross estate.

Of course, the purpose of the alternate valuation date is to permit a reduction in estate taxes whenever there is a decrease in the aggregate value of the estate property. However, there are some interrelated income tax consequences that should be evaluated before selecting the most advantageous valuation date, especially since the alternate valuation date may not be elected unless the valuation amount decreases both the value of the gross estate and the estate tax liability of the estate. The election may not be used to maximize the use of the unified credit and step-up basis of property to heirs.

Income earned subsequent to death but prior to the alternate valuation date is not included in the gross estate. Such property includes post-death interest accrued on interest-bearing obligations, rental payments accrued after the date of death and before the subsequent valuation date, and ordinary dividends out of earnings and profits declared to shareholders of record after the date of the decedent's death. One district court indicates that proceeds from the sale of oil and gas during the alternate valuation period is not includable in the gross estate.

Even when a decedent's will directs the executor to sell assets to a specified individual for less than an adequate and full consideration, the assets are includable in the decedent's gross estate at their fair market value on the applicable valuation date.

While the alternate valuation date election may be appropriate for anyone, the next key is of particular interest to farmers and owners of closely-held businesses.

20

SPECIAL-USE VALUATION

A special-use valuation is available in the case of property being used for farming purposes or closely held businesses. Any property so qualified may be valued at the fair market value of its actual use rather than any speculative value (that is, "highest and best" use) that it might have. This special valuation process may be used to reduce the value of an estate by as much as $750,000. For example, if a decedent's estate contains special-use property that is valued at $2.3 million at its highest-and-best use, but only at $1.2 million at its current use, the estate would be valued at $1.55 million ($2.3 million less $750,000).

In order to qualify for this special-use valuation, several tests must be met:

1. The value of the closely held business or farm must be at least 50% of the adjusted value of the gross estate (determined on the basis of its highest-and-best use).
2. The value of the real property must be 25% of the adjusted value of the gross estate.
3. The property must be located in the United States.
4. The property must pass to a qualified heir (e.g., family).
5. The real property must have been used by the decedent or a member of his/her family as a farm or other closely held business, and the decedent or a member of his/her family must have participated materially in its operation during five out of the eight years preceding his/her death. This

special method probably cannot be used for real property that the decedent has rented.

The formula for computing this current special-use value for farmland may be shown as follows:

$$SUV = \frac{R - T}{I}$$

SUV = Current special-use value

R = Average annual gross cash rent per acre for comparable farming land in the same locality

T = Average annual state and local real estate taxes per acre for comparable land

I = Average annual effective interest rate for all new federal bank loans

There is no special-use valuation for purposes of valuing property for the lifetime-gift provision.

For closely held business property or farm property where comparable land cannot be found, Section 2032 A (e)(8) provides several methods of valuation based primarily on the capitalization of income.

A dual election of the AVD and the special use valuation (SUV) is allowable. Further, community property is treated in the same manner as separate property. Therefore, if property is held by a decedent and spouse as community property, the entire value of the property is taken into consideration.

Tax benefits of SUV are recaptured if, within ten years after the decedent's death but before the death of the qualified heir, such heir either disposes of any interest in the property to a nonfamily member or ceases to use the property for the qualified use. A cessation of qualified use also triggers recapture. In general, the recapture amount is the excess of the estate tax liability that would have been paid had the SUV not been elected over the estate tax paid based on SUV. Be careful, because the IRS insists that the procedural aspects of an SUV election be followed closely.

21

TAX BASIS FOR HEIRS

For estates and heirs of decedents, the basis of inherited property is stepped up (or stepped down) to the property's value at the time of the decedent's death—or six months later if the alternative valuation date is elected. Thus, if an heir sells the property shortly after inheriting it, there will be little or no income tax due, even though the property might have appreciated in value substantially while owned by the decedent. This advantage is a very important concept in tax planning.

If the executor or administrator of the estate elected to value the property for tax purposes at a date six months after the decedent's death, the asset's basis will be the value at such alternative valuation date. Where the special-use valuation is elected for property used for farming purposes or closely-held businesses, such lower value is the basis of the inherited assets.

For example, suppose the decedent died on January 12, 1993, and his will directs the executor to transfer a certain asset to a beneficiary. This asset had a fair market value of $500,000 at the decedent's date of death. On April 13, 1993, the property was distributed to this beneficiary, at which time the property had a fair market value of $450,000. Assuming that no election is made by the executor, this asset is included in the gross estate at $500,000, and the beneficiary receives a $500,000 stepped-up basis. If the executor elects the alternative valuation method under Section 2032, the included value of the asset is $450,000 with a stepped-up basis to the beneficiary of $450,000.

A carryover basis was available to certain taxpayers

dying between January 1, 1977, and November 7, 1978. President Clinton has indicated that he would consider taxing capital gains at death. Therefore, some form of carryover basis rather than step-up basis may be passed during the Clinton Administration.

The basis of appreciated property acquired by gift within one year of death is not adjusted to its fair market value at date of death if it returns to the donor or the donor's spouse.

Because substantial income tax savings may result, any assets that have increased in value—especially if the taxpayer is elderly—should be retained until death so that the heirs will receive the step-up basis.

The death of an individual eliminates any potential depreciation recapture. Regulations indicate that the depreciation adjustment acquired from a decedent is zero, assuming the basis is determined under Section 1014(a).

Under the Clinton Administration, the investment tax credit may be resurrected. Pursuant to prior law, investment credit property was treated more favorably than recapture-property credit is treated. Under that law, there was no investment credit recapture when the estate or beneficiary disposed of the assets that would have given the decedent an investment credit recapture.

In the next key, we discuss how to calculate the taxable estate and how to compute the estate tax liability.

22

TAXABLE ESTATE AND ESTATE TAX

From the gross estate there are deducted (1) indebtedness such as mortgages and loans owed by the decedent; (2) expenses incurred and paid during administration, such as attorneys' fees and court costs; (3) taxes, principally income taxes and property taxes, during administration (not federal estate and gift taxes and not state death taxes); and (4) casualty losses incurred during administration of the estate. The resulting figure is the amount of the adjusted gross estate. The sole object of the calculation of the amount of the adjusted gross estate is to determine the amount, if any, of a marital deduction. Then there are deducted any marital deduction and any charitable contributions, resulting in the taxable estate.

Next there must be added to the amount of the taxable estate any taxable gifts made in 1977 and later years, but not gifts in contemplation of death. These are called *adjusted taxable gifts.* Values used are those of the dates of the gifts, and the amounts of gift taxes paid are ignored. At this point, the "tentative tax base" is reached, to reflect the cumulative nature of the computation.

To the amount of the tentative tax base (taxable estate plus adjusted taxable gifts), the unified tax rate table is applied. The result is the amount of the tentative estate tax. The next deduction is for gift taxes paid on gifts made after 1976. The resulting amount is called the tax before unified credit. A unified credit is then deducted.

From the balance the following credits for any taxes paid of the following types are deducted:

1. State death taxes.
2. Gift taxes paid on gifts made before 1977 where the subject of the gift is included in the gross estate.
3. Foreign death taxes.
4. Estate taxes on prior transfers to decedent from a transferor decedent who dies within 10 years before, or within 2 years after, this decedent's death.

The resulting amount is the estate tax payable. The federal estate tax return and a check for the tax are due within nine months after death, with possible extensions of time, if applied for before the due date.

23

MARITAL DEDUCTION

Investment assets and other property left by a decedent to a surviving spouse qualify for a marital deduction. The interest bequeathed must be a nonterminable one (except for a qualified terminable interest property [QTIP] trust). In other words, suppose the wife is the survivor. If she dies before all installments of an obligation are paid to her, the balance must go to her heirs or otherwise as she alone directs. If the survivor's interest is only a life estate, it does not qualify (unless it is a QTIP trust). If the interest is as a beneficiary of a trust, she must have a general power of appointment so that she can take out any or all of the cash and property at any time and for any reason. Further, she must be able under her will to bequeath any trust corpus not distributed to her during her life to her estate or any entity she wishes.

There is an unlimited estate tax marital deduction available for property passing to a surviving spouse (including community property). This unlimited marital deduction has at least one advantage: If no estate planning has occurred before the first spouse dies, there is still time. The bad news is that if all of the assets are left to the surviving spouse, the survivor may be pushed into a much higher estate tax bracket. Of course, as long as the surviving spouse marries a younger partner and then dies first, a new generation-skipping technique may develop. An interesting legal possibility is that as long as each surviving spouse marries "young," dies first, and there are no simultaneous deaths, assets could theoretically escape the estate tax indefinitely.

Only the net amount of property that passes to the surviving spouse is allowed as a marital deduction. For example, if property is transferred to a surviving spouse and such property is subject to a liability, then only the net value of the asset is allowable as a deduction. Also, the marital deduction is net of any applicable federal or state estate or death taxes.

For example, suppose W, a surviving spouse, receives a residence appraised at $280,000, which is subject to a mortgage of $160,000. The marital deduction is limited to the net value passing to the surviving spouse, or $120,000.

The growth in the area of marital deduction trusts has been high since 1981 because of the QTIP trust. This type of trust essentially gives the estate the best of both worlds:

1. An after-death choice of letting the spouse use what he/she needs, while
2. At the same time qualifying for the marital deduction.

These trusts require technical precision and should be prepared by an estate planning counsel. (See Key 45). The marital deduction is not available to a non-resident alien.

24

ADMINISTRATION AND FUNERAL EXPENSES

The gross estate is reduced by all allowable deductions. In a community property state, if the expenditures are chargeable against both halves of the community property, only one-half of the expenses are deductible.

A deduction is granted to the extent allowable under local law for funeral expenses. Funeral expenses include a reasonable expenditure for a tombstone, monument, burial lot, and the cost of transportation of the person taking the body to the place of burial. Reasonable expenses include expenditures for the future care of a mausoleum. In order for a deduction to be allowable as a funeral expense, the expenditures cannot exceed the value of the property included in the decedent's gross estate.

All reasonable and necessary expenses incurred in the administration of the decedent's estate are deductible from the gross estate. The administration of the estate includes the collection of the assets, the payment of debts, and the distribution of property to the proper beneficiaries. The three types of administrative expenses are executor's commissions, attorney's fees, and miscellaneous expenses.

An executor normally is named by a decedent in his will. If there is no will, the state court will appoint an administrator. The executor manages the estate's personal property and real estate; collects assets; pays debts, administrative expenses, and funeral expenses; and distributes the remainder according to the will.

Selection of a well-qualified executor is enormously important.

A deduction for executor's commissions is allowed to the extent that such an amount has actually been paid or for an amount which at the time of the filing of the estate tax return may reasonably be expected to be paid, but no deduction is allowed if the commission is not collected. When the executor is also a major beneficiary, he may wish not to receive a commission because it is taxable as ordinary income. (Many people forget to report this income and are caught by the IRS.) Instead, the executor may wish to receive a larger share of inheritance, which is not taxable to the executor. A mechanism should be placed in the will for the executor to disclaim any commission, if so desired.

Attorney fees actually paid or reasonably expected to be paid are deductible. These attorney fees do not include charges incurred by beneficiaries incident to litigation as to their respective interests.

Miscellaneous administrative expenses include court costs, surrogate's fees, clerk hire, and similar charges. All expenses necessarily incurred in preserving and distributing the estate are deductible, including the cost of storing or maintaining property of the estate when immediate distribution to the beneficiaries is impossible. Lawsuits to enforce the terms of a will may be taken as an expense of the estate. For example, "I want my house sold and the proceeds equally divided." Here a suit to do so and/or sales commissions would be deductible.

Expenditures that are not essential for the proper settlement of the estate, but that are incurred for the individual benefit of heirs, legatees, or devisees, are not deductible (e.g., broker's commission on sale of house by surviving spouse because house is too large). However, expenses for selling property of the estate are deductible if the sale is necessary in order to pay the decedent's debts, expenses of administration, or taxes, to preserve the estate; or to effect distribution.

Under Section 642(g), expenditures may not be used to offset the sales price of assets for income tax purposes unless a waiver of the right to deduct such an item on the federal estate tax return is filed.

The next key discusses a charitable deduction that can reduce your taxes.

25

CHARITABLE
CONTRIBUTIONS

An estate or gift tax deduction is available for bequests to qualified charitable organizations. If death taxes are payable out of the charitable bequest, then the deductible amount is net of such taxes. Further, the charitable deduction may not exceed the value of the transferred property required to be included in the gross estate.

The law does not allow a deduction for bequests other than to charitable organizations and to the surviving spouse (i.e., marital deduction). Thus, other specific bequests in the will to certain individuals are not deductible.

Gifts made to religious, charitable, scientific, literary, and educational organizations are normally deductible. Gifts made to a public institution are deductible if they are made to the United States, any state, territory, any political subdivision thereof, or the District of Columbia.

A citizen or resident is allowed an estate or gift tax deduction for transfers to a charitable organization, regardless of whether it is a U.S. institution. On the other hand, a nonresident alien may obtain a deduction only for gifts to a domestic corporation and may not deduct gifts to a foreign trust, community chest, fund, or foundation unless the gift is used within the United States for charitable purposes.

A charitable deduction is allowed for certain future interests in property given to a charity. The future interest (except for a future interest in a personal residence or farm) must be in the form of a charitable remainder annuity trust, a charitable remainder unitrust, or a pooled-income fund.

Charitable remainder annuity trust (GRAT). This future interest is a trust that is to pay its income beneficiary (or beneficiaries) a specific sum that is not less than 5% of the initial fair market value of all property placed in the trust. At the death of the income beneficiary, or at the end of a term of years (not greater than 20 years), the remainder interest must be paid to a qualified organization described above.

Charitable remainder unitrust (GRUT). This future interest is a trust that is to pay the income beneficiary (or beneficiaries) a fixed percentage that is not less than 5% of the net fair market value of its assets (as valued annually). There are two exceptions. The trust instrument may provide (1) that for any year, the trustee is to pay the income beneficiary the amount of trust income where this amount is less than the portion required to be distributed by the particular unitrust, and (2) that the trustee is to pay the beneficiary an amount of trust income in excess of that required to be distributed, to the extent that he/she paid less than that portion in prior years because of the requirement to pay only the amount of the trust income.

A GRAT provides for a guaranteed fixed-income payment based upon the value of the assets at the time they are initially transferred to the irrevocable trust. A GRUT provides for income payments as a percentage of the annual fair market value of the trust. The grantor transfers ownership of the assets to the trust and receives a charitable deduction equal to the present value of the trust's remainder interest. The good news is that the grantor enjoys use of the transferred assets, obtains a charitable deduction, avoids probate, and has a reduced estate at death.

If anyone other than the grantor or spouse is an income beneficiary, there will be a taxable gift equal to the present value of the income interest. On the death of the last income beneficiary, the assets pass to the appropriate charity. If the trustee sells any of the assets, the charitable remainder trust does not pay any capital gains tax.

Huge estate tax savings are possible by the use of a qualified personal residence GRIT. The grantor transfers the residence to a trust, with the right to use the residence for a specific number of years. The grantor's spouse can remain in the house for life. Afterward, ownership passes to the designated beneficiaries, often the children. The house goes to the beneficiaries at a deep discount from existing values for purposes of the gift tax. Furthermore, future appreciation is not included in the grantor's estate. Finally, unlike GRUTS and GRATS, the grantor's estate is not increased by annuity payments.

Pooled-income fund. This future interest is similar to a charitable remainder trust except that the donor's irrevocable gifts are commingled with similar contributions in a fund maintained by the organization to which the remainder interest is contributed.

An individual may establish a charitable income trust (often called a charitable lead trust), give away some of the income from the property, and still keep the property. A charitable income trust must be either an annuity trust or unitrust.

A *charitable remainder trust* is the opposite. The donor retains the income from some property and gives away the entire principal. A remainder trust must be in the form of an annuity trust, a unitrust, or a pooled-income trust. For both a charitable income trust and charitable remainder trust, a donor receives a current income tax deduction that is equal to the present value of the interest in the asset given to the charity (using 10% present worth annuity tables).

One other exception to this denial of a charitable deduction (where the donor retains a life interest in the property) applies to gifts of personal residences and farms. A donor may still obtain a charitable deduction for a gift to a publicly supported charity (but not to a trust) even while retaining a right to live in the residence or use the farm. However, the law does severely restrict the contribution of future interest in personal property (for example, paintings, jewelry, antiques) where the donor wishes to retain the enjoyment of the property during his/her lifetime. Further, some contributions of tangible personal property to public charities result in a 50% reduction in the appreciation portion of the property.

Under an annuity trust, the trust is established to pay a guaranteed annuity to a charity. The annuity can be expressed in a stated dollar amount or a percentage of the initial amount given to the trust. For example, it could be $100,000 per year or 5% of the initial $2 million trust. The purpose of the trust is to minimize or eliminate the taxable gift and prevent the trust assets from being included in the grantor's estate. The annuity trust is quite attractive for transferring assets that are difficult to value (e.g., closely-held businesses or oil and gas reserves). The deductible amount for both types of trusts is based upon tables that assume 120% of the applicable midterm rate.

Under a unitrust, a qualified unitrust interest is paid to the charity—expressed as a percentage of the fair market value of the trust property, determined annually. For example, if the adjusted payout is 7% and the trust assets increase in value from $1 million to $2 million, the annual payment to the charity will increase from $70,000 to $140,000. In general, a unitrust will produce a greater deduction than an annuity trust with the same payout requirement. Bear in mind that a private foundation can be the charitable beneficiary of the lead interest.

The next key outlines the various credits that can reduce estate taxes.

26

HELPFUL CREDITS

The gross estate tax is computed by using the unified rate schedule. These rates, which apply to citizens and residents of the United States, range from 18% on the first $10,000 to 55% on the entire taxable estate in excess of $3 million. The tax computed at these rates, however, is subject to reduction by various credits allowed on account of other taxes. Some of the credits allowed as deductions from the gross estate tax are state death tax credit, a credit for tax on prior transfers, credit for foreign death taxes, and the unified estate and gift tax credit.

A credit is allowed against the federal estate tax for the amount of any state estate, inheritance, legacy, or succession taxes actually paid with respect to any property included in the decedent's gross estate. Every state except Nevada imposes some form of death taxes, either an inheritance tax, an estate tax, or both. If the decedent's taxable estate does not exceed $40,000, there is no credit allowed for *state* death taxes. If the taxable estate exceeds $40,000, the credit is limited by an amount determined by a table in Section 2011(b). The adjusted taxable estate is the taxable estate less $60,000.

The credit for state death taxes is limited to those taxes that were actually paid. Basically, the credit must be claimed within four years after the filing of the estate tax return for the decedent's estate.

Since a credit is allowed only up to the amount of state taxes paid, care should be taken to supply the required information in full. This is particularly important when a deposit is made with the state as security for the payment of the state tax. It is also important when discounts or refunds may be allowed by the state. The information to be furnished to the district director should disclose the total amount of tax imposed by the state, the amount of any discount allowed, the total amount actually paid in cash, and the identity of the property for which the state tax has been paid or is to be paid.

Postmortem estate planning is possible with state death taxes. Instead of claiming state death taxes (imposed on a transfer for public, charitable, or religious uses) as credit, an executor may elect to deduct these expenditures.

For all or a part of the estate tax paid with respect to the transfer of property to the decedent by someone who died within ten years before or within two years after the decedent's death, a credit is allowed against the estate tax. The credit for tax on prior transfers is allowed only for prior estate taxes, not gift taxes. Also, within limits, it is allowed for more than two successive decedents. If the transferor died within two years before or after the present decedent's death, the credit allowed for the tax is 100% of the maximum amount allowable. If the transferor predeceased the decedent by more than two years, the credit allowable is reduced by 20% for each full two years by which the death of the transferor preceded that of the present decedent.

The credit for tax on prior transfers is limited to the smaller of the following amounts:

1. An amount that bears the same ratio to the transferor's adjusted federal estate tax as the value of the transferred property bears to the transferor's adjusted taxable estate.

2. The amount by which the estate tax of the present decedent as determined without regard to a credit on prior transfers exceeds the estate tax for his/her estate as determined by excluding from the gross estate the net value of the transfer.

Since many other countries levy death taxes on the transfer by nonresident aliens of property situated within their boundaries, the estates of some U.S.

citizens are subject to double taxes. However, the federal government has entered into estate tax conventions with a number of foreign countries to provide relief from such double taxation. The credit for foreign death taxes is limited to the smaller of a particular limitation or a general limitation. The *particular limitation* limits the credit to the share of the foreign tax paid for property located in the foreign country. Under the *general limitation,* this credit cannot exceed the gross federal estate tax less credits for state death taxes and federal gift taxes attributable to property located in the foreign country. This is a complicated area and anyone trying to use this credit should seek counsel.

The *unified credit* for both the estate tax and the gift tax is $192,800. The equivalent exemption of $600,000 is the amount of the taxable estate that passes free of the unified estate tax at death. In other words, a unified credit of $192,800 will allow approximately $600,000 to escape the federal estate tax. Legislation has been introduced in Congress to reduce this credit to only $54,800 (i.e., only taxable estates up to $200,000 would be exempt).

This credit (like the other credits) is deducted directly from the gross estate tax to determine the net estate tax payable. The net estate tax payable is the amount that becomes due to the Internal Revenue Service within nine months after the death unless an extension of time is granted.

To be allowed, another credit for *gift tax paid* must be claimed within four years after the filing of the estate tax return. Since under the law taxable gifts made after December 31, 1976, become part of the tax base and thus subject to the tax rate, any gift tax rate paid on gifts made after December 31, 1976, may be subtracted from the gross estate tax. Thus, in essence, the tax paid on such gifts becomes a credit against the estate tax.

The next key discusses how to postpone the payment of the estate tax liability.

27

DEFERRAL OF TAX LIABILITY

There is a 15-year installment provision for a qualifying interest in a closely held business or farm. An executor may defer all payments of tax for five years and pay only interest for such period. For years 6 through 15 after the decedent's death, the tax is payable in equal installments. A low 4% interest rate applies to the first $345,800 of estate tax (less the available unified credit).

In order to qualify, the interest in the closely held business (proprietor, partner, and stockholder) must exceed 35% of the decedent's adjusted gross estate (AGE). AGE refers to gross estate less expenses, debts, claims, and losses (so-called Sections 2053 and 2054 expenses), but before marital and charitable deductions. In order to qualify, it may be worthwhile to give securities or other property to heir(s) before death in order to make sure that the required proportion of the estate consists of farm or business property. Further, a taxpayer may wish to delay giving children a share of the family business before he/she dies.

An interest in a closely held business refers to

1. An interest as a proprietor in a trade or business.
2. An interest as a partner in a partnership where 20% or more of the total capital interest in such partnership is included in determining the gross estate of the decedent or the partnership has 15 or fewer partners.
3. Stock in a corporation where 20% or more is included in the gross estate or the corporation has 15 or fewer shareholders.
4. Indirect ownership of a closely held business

interest through a holding company. However, such holding company stock must have no market value on a stock exchange or on an over-the-counter market at the time of the decedent's death. (Here, however, the five-year deferral and 4% interest rate are not available; only the ten-year installment payments are available).

In order to determine the value of any interest in a closely held business, the value of its passive assets is *not* includable. A passive asset is any asset other than an asset used in carrying on a trade or business. For example, suppose a corporation owns real estate not used in the business. The value of the decedent's stock attributable to this passive asset must be eliminated in order to determine if the decedent's stock meets the 35% test.

Under this five-year deferral and ten-year installment payment plan, any interest payable by the estate on deferred payments is deductible as an administrative expense under Section 2053 for purposes of determining taxable estate and estate taxes. Thus, this deduction can have a significant impact on directly and indirectly reducing the estate tax. The stock interest in two or more businesses may be aggregated for testing purposes (that is, the 35% test) where the decedent owned 20% or more of the outstanding stock of each corporation.

The payment of the estate tax is accelerated if one third or more of a decedent's qualifying interest is disposed of or if there is a withdrawal of money (or other property) in an amount equal to one third of the value of the decedent's interest. A redemption under Section 303 is excepted from this acceleration.

A disposition of holding company stock (which is treated as business company stock) or the withdrawal of money or other property from the holding company is treated as a fatal disposition or withdrawal (i.e., acceleration of the estate tax).

Where an election is made to pay taxes in installments under Section 6166, a special lien procedure may be elected so that an executor will not be personally liable for the taxes. The executor and all beneficiaries with an interest in the qualifying property must file a written agreement, consenting to the creation of a lien, and must designate a responsible person to deal with the IRS as an agent for the appropriate parties. Never miss an installment because the tax liability is accelerated and the loss of the beneficial interest rate can be costly.

The next series of keys discusses a similar tax—a gift tax on the right to transfer property to someone else. Gift-giving is an excellent estate planning strategy.

28

DEFINITION OF A GIFT

An effective vehicle of transfer in estate planning is a system of lifetime gifts, which eliminate all probate and administration expenses on the property transferred. Gifts may reduce estate taxes because the amount of income that would have been accumulated from the property is removed from the transferor's gross estate. The use of a gift provides savings in income taxes when the income is shifted from the high tax bracket of the transferor into the low tax bracket of the transferee.

Of course, the use of gifts produces many advantages other than taxes. They may be used to continue control of a business within the family or to serve specific desires estate owners have for their children. Gifts, like all other devices, have their costs; the most significant cost of making a gift is the complete loss of control of the asset. Of course, with the unified tax structure, the use of gifts as an estate planning tool has lost some of its appeal. Furthermore, the new "kiddie tax" on unearned income of children under age 14 is calculated at the custodial parent's marginal tax rate.

Since making gifts is an obvious method of avoiding the estate tax, the government imposes a tax on gift transfers in order to partially plug this escape route. However, you can still make gifts without incurring this tax. You are allowed to make tax-free gifts of $10,000 per person during each year, plus use up your unified credit at any time during your life. Further, if spouses consent on the gift tax return to split their gifts, all gifts to third parties are considered as having been made one-half by each spouse. You may find it advantageous to make gifts as time goes by.

The federal gift tax is a progressive tax levied upon transfer of gifts from one person (donor) to another person (donee). The donor is primarily liable for this tax. The difference between a gift and an inheritance is that a gift is the transmission of property from one living person to another. To further qualify as a gift, property must be given without any consideration with no strings attached.

The establishment of the gift tax prevents people from avoiding the progressive federal estate tax by distributing assets during their lifetime. An interesting note is that, although the yield of this tax and the dollar value of gifts are relatively small, lifetime giving is almost universal among people with substantial wealth.

The statutes fail to give an exact definition of a gift. As set forth by Section 2511(a), the gift tax applies "whether the transfer is in trust or otherwise, whether the gift is direct or indirect, and whether the property is real or personal, tangible or intangible." The Tax Court has stipulated that the six following items are essential elements of a bona fide gift:

1. A donor competent to make a gift.
2. A donee capable of taking the gift.
3. A clear and unmistakable intention on the part of the donor to absolutely and irrevocably divest himself of the title, dominion, and control of the subject matter of the gift in presents.
4. There is an actual irrevocable transfer of the present legal title and of the dominion and control of the entire gift to the donee, so that the donor can exercise no further active dominion or control over it.
5. A delivery to the donee of the subject of the gift or of the most effective means of commanding the dominion of it.
6. Acceptance of the gift by the donee.

Gift tax returns are filed and taxes paid on a

calendar-year basis on April 15 following the year of transfers. However, for a deceased donor, the gift tax return must be filed no later than the date for filing the federal estate tax return (which is generally nine months after the date of death).

In general, a gift is valued at its fair market value on the date of the gift. There is no alternate valuation date as there is for estate tax purposes. Where property is transferred for less than adequate and full consideration, then the amount by which the fair market value of property exceeds the value of the consideration is deemed to be a gift.

There is the practical side to gift giving. People should be careful not to give away too much of an estate. Otherwise there may not be enough money for the sometimes horrendous expenses of old age.

(See also Key 31, INCOMPLETE GIFTS.)

29

ANNUAL EXCLUSIONS

A donor may exclude from the gift tax up to $10,000 per donee per year. This excluded amount is over and beyond the available unified credit. A married couple electing to split gifts can exclude $20,000 of present-interest gifts per year for each donee. Further, there is an unlimited exclusion for amounts paid for the benefit of a donee for certain medical-care expenses and bona fide school tuition. The donee does not have to be related to the donor. Medical or tuition "gifts" must be made to the service provider (rather than the donee).

There is no $10,000 annual exclusion for gifts considered to be *future interests.* In order to have a present interest in property, an individual must currently have the right to use, possess, or enjoy the property. There must be a substantial present economic benefit for the person to have a present interest and qualify for the annual exclusion.

By gift splitting, a husband and wife may combine their annual exclusions and unified credits. Combining the annual exclusion and the unified credits, the gift-splitting election allows a donor to transfer a great deal of property to family members and thereby escape the federal estate tax. For example, a husband and wife could transfer $2.4 million of tax-free gifts to their three children and their children's spouses over a ten-year period.

You may wish to consider a transfer under the Gifts of Securities to Minors Act. In a typical situation, the donor irrevocably transfers assets to a minor by registering the property in the name of a custodian designated by the donor. To be sure the property will not be included in the donor's estate, the donor should not be the custodian. Make your spouse or someone else the custodian.

The donor must be able to prove that gifts are in fact made. For example, one father wished to leave several of his ivory figurines to each of his minor children. He identified the figurines by clearly placing each child's initials under various figurines contained in his collection. But all of the figurines continued to remain in his safe deposit box. Here the Internal Revenue Service refused to agree that the gifts had in fact been completed.

Before making lifetime gifts, it must be remembered that, under certain circumstances, the gift property may later be included in the donor's gross estate along with a gross-up of the gift taxes even though they were made during the donor's lifetime. Without adequate and full consideration of this tax risk, any transfers of certain types of property made by the decedent within three years of death are interpreted as having been made in contemplation of death. Thus, such property and gift tax gross-ups are included in the donor's gross estate. Likewise, the relinquishment of a power over property transferred during lifetime, or the exercise or release of a *power of appointment,* within three years before death is deemed to have been made in contemplation of death.

As people become older and the value of their assets increases, a program of lifetime gifts may be beneficial. Let us assume that a wealthy married man in a high tax bracket plans to leave a portion of his estate to his children. If the father's estate surpasses the exemption-equivalent level, and if the children who receive the gifts are in a low tax bracket, it may be advantageous for him to make gifts while he is still living. Since the children will eventually receive the assets anyway, it makes sense for the father to distribute them in the most advantageous manner. Although it is usually beneficial to make gifts, many people do not use this valuable tax-planning tool.

In most cases it will benefit the taxpayer to take the unified credit as soon as possible. The federal gift tax is progressive and cumulative, and there is no valid reason for saving portions of the credit for future years. If portions of the unified credit are saved for future periods, gift tax rates might be less and therefore would reflect an illusory tax savings. But if one considers the loss of earning power of gift taxes paid immediately as the result of any "saved" credit, then this saving will be deceptive, and the net result will probably be an economic loss. The concept of the time value of money seems appropriate here in that money (or gifts) received today are likely to be worth more than the same amount received at some future date.

30

PRESENT VERSUS FUTURE INTEREST GIFTS

Earlier, the criticality of determining whether a gift is a present or future interest was mentioned. This topic deserves a more thorough discussion. The definition of a present interest is an unrestricted right to the immediate use, possession, or enjoyment of property or the income from property (such as a life estate or term certain).

The entire amount of any gift of future interest in property must be included in taxable gifts, with the exception of certain gifts to minors (discussed later in more detail). Reversions, remainders, and other interests or estates, whether vested or contingent, and whether or not supported by a particular interest or estate, which are limited to commence in use, possession, or enjoyment at some future date or time, are all included in the term future interest. From a decree by the Supreme Court we find that the critical test is whether there has been a postponement of the rights of the donees to use, possess, and enjoy the property. The law has stipulated that any remainder interest, even though marketable, is a future interest.

It is advisable, then, to make sure that the gifts made are of a present interest if it is expected that any exclusions from the amounts of these gifts will be taken. Gifts of present interest are the only form of gifts to which an exclusion can be applied. The classification of gifts as either present or future interest should be made prior to the gift by the donor so as to take the optimum advantage of the tax consequences.

For example, an unmarried person transfers assets to a trust for Sam for life, with the remainder to John. Sam's life estate value is $2700, and John's remainder interest is worth $9300. The taxable gift is $9300 because there is no exclusion on the future-interest gift.

One important exception to the future-interest rule is a transfer under the Uniform Gift to Minors Act. In a typical situation, a taxpayer irrevocably transfers securities, cash, or life insurance to a minor by registering the property in the name of the custodian or guardian designated by the donor. The donor should not be the custodian so as to ensure that the given property will not be included in the donor's gross estate if he/she dies before the minor reaches the age of majority. This selection can be a very important event, since the law indicates that if the donor is the custodian and dies before the donee has reached the age of 21 years, it is quite likely that the gift will be included in the gross estate of the donor.

This exception to the future-interest rule will be the case if all three of the following conditions are met:

1. Both the property and its income may be expended by or for the benefit of the donee before he/she attains the age of 21.

2. Any portion of the property and its income not disposed of under condition 1 will pass to the donee when he/she attains the age of 21 years.

3. Any portion of the property and income not disposed of under condition 1 will be payable either to the estate of the donee or to whomever the donee may appoint under a general power of appointment if he/she dies before attaining the age of 21 years.

In essence, the first condition means that the trust instrument must not impose any substantial restrictions on the trustee's ability to determine the amount of income or property distributed and the purposes for which the expenditures are made. A trustee, however, may be required to consider the donee-beneficiary's other available resources before distributing any principal or income to the donee. A gift qualifies for the annual exclusion where the restrictions in the trust instrument are no greater than the restrictions imposed on a guardian by the state law. The trustee also can be instructed to invest solely in life insurance policies.

The second condition requires any corpus and accumulated income to pass to the donee at age 21. A donor who does not wish to distribute the principal to the beneficiary at age 21 can give the assets to a ten-year reversionary trust, with the income earned in the trust to be distributed to a Section 2503(c) trust for the donee. The accumulated income qualifies as a present interest until the donee reaches 21, and the donor can obtain the corpus property after ten years.

If a donee dies before age 21, the trust corpus and income must be payable to the donee's estate or to someone the donee may appoint under a general power of appointment. By giving a donee the power to demand the trust property for a reasonable period of time after reaching age 21, the trust may continue beyond the donee's twenty-first birthday. However, the donee must have a general power of appointment over the trust income/corpus or the property must pass automatically to the donee's estate.

For example, a mother transfers securities worth $90,000 to a trust for the benefit of her son. The property and income may be expended by or for the benefit of the minor prior to his attaining 21 years of age and, if not so expended, will pass to the donee upon his attaining majority, or in the event of his prior death, will be payable to his estate or to whomever he may appoint under a general power of appointment. Assuming gift-splitting, the minimum taxable gift (ignoring the unified credit) is $70,000 ($90,000 − $20,000).

There are four areas where a lifetime gift does not remove the property from the gross estate. Key 31 covers these incomplete gifts.

31

INCOMPLETE GIFTS

A major objective of a lifetime gift is to remove the property from the gross estate of the donor. There are four major areas where this objective is not accomplished, since the gift is included in the donor's taxable estate:

- *gifts in contemplation of death*
- *transfers with a retained life interest*
- *transfers taking effect at death*
- *revocable transfers*

Many transfers that are not complete for estate tax purposes may be complete for gift tax purposes. They are "not always mutually exclusive."

Although no gift tax is due until a gift is complete, when a donor makes a transfer that he believes to be an incomplete gift because of a retained power over the property, the transfer still must be disclosed on the gift tax form (Form 709). Such disclosure must be made in the year of transfer along with all relevant facts, including a copy of the instrument of transfer.

A decedent's gross estate is increased by the fair market value of certain gifts in contemplation of death. Prior to 1977, gifts made within three years prior to the date of the decedent's death were presumed to be made in contemplation of death. Even if the property is sold by the donee before the donor's death, the fair market value of the same property at the date of death is included. Any increase in value resulting from actions of the donee is not taken into consideration when determining the value. However, if the donee has dissipated the property so that there is little left on the date of the transferor's death, the amount includable is not what actually exists, but rather is the present value of the property originally transferred.

In order to overcome the three-year presumption, the administrator must show by a fair preponderance of evidence that the donor had life motives rather than death motives for making the gifts. If the donor lived three years after making a gift, it was assumed that the gift was not in contemplation of death, and it is not included in the gross estate.

Under the present law, the three-year rule about gifts in contemplation of death applies only to certain property for decedents dying after December 31, 1981. This property (sometimes referred to as Section 2035(b)(2) property) must be covered by:

Section 2036. Retained life estate.
Section 2037. Transfers taking effect at death.
Section 2038. Revocable transfers.
Section 2041. Powers of appointment.
Section 2042. Life insurance.

In other words, two or more sections must operate together (i.e., a release of a prior retained life estate within three years before death).

Also, gifts made within three years of death are included for purposes of qualifying for *special-use valuation* under Section 2032A (see Key 20), for deferred payment of estate taxes under Section 6166, for qualified redemptions to pay estate taxes under Section 303, (see Key 27), and for estate tax liens under Subchapter C of Chapter 64.

Thus, deathbed gifts of cash and certain property should be a popular means of estate planning. For example, a person may give an unlimited number of less-than-$10,000 gifts on the deathbed, and any such gifts are removed from the gross estate. The exemption applies to gifts within three years of death only if no gift tax return was required. For maximum tax benefit, however, be careful to avoid deathbed gifts of the five categories just listed, such as life insurance.

Even when it appears that a gift may be in contemplation of death, a gift may still be advisable. The donor may live three years; if not, he may be in a high income tax bracket and the transfer can place the income-producing property in the hands of a lower-tax-bracket donee. Moreover, any gift tax paid is normally allowed as a full credit against any future estate tax, even if a spouse elects under Section 2513 to split a gift in contemplation of death. In other words, the gift tax paid with respect to both halves of the gift is allowed as a credit on the donor's (decedent's) estate tax return, but there is no restoration of the unified credit used against gift taxes paid by the surviving spouse.

For a discussion of the other three incomplete gifts, see RETAINED LIFE ESTATE (Key 13), DEATH TRANSFERS (Key 14), and REVOCABLE TRANSFERS (Key 15).

In the next key, we see how to put many of the preceding concepts together to compute the gift-tax liability.

32

COMPUTING GIFT TAX

Although the gift tax is imposed separately in each calendar year on the total taxable gifts made during a given year, the applicable tax payable is determined by the total of all gifts made by the donor during that year and in all prior years. That is, the gift tax rates are cumulative and progressive. From the standpoint of gift tax rate alone, there is no benefit gained by spreading gifts over a number of years; however, it may be beneficial to spread gifts over a number of years in order to take advantage of the $10,000 annual exclusion and other deductions. There are six major steps in computing the gift tax payable.

Step 1: Determine the amount (fair market value, FMV) of the taxable gifts for the calendar year for which the gift tax return is being prepared. This step is broken down into a formula, outlined below.

Step 2: Ascertain the total FMV of all taxable gifts made by the donor for all prior calendar years.

Step 3: Sum the amounts in steps 1 and 2. Compute the tax on this total by using the unified estate and gift tax rates.

Step 4: Compute the theoretical unified gift tax on the amount in step 2.

Step 5: Subtract the tax computed in step 4 from the tax computed in step 3 in order to determine the tentative gift tax payable.

Step 6: Subtract the applicable unified credit from the amount in step 5 to arrive at the gift tax payable.

Step 1 above can be expanded into this formula:

Gross gifts (FMV)		XX
Less:		
Annual exclusions, if any, of $10,000 per donee per year of present-interest gifts		X
		XX
Less other deductions:		
FMV of charitable gifts	X	
Marital deduction on gifts to spouse	X	X
Taxable gifts		XX

Notice that pre-1977 gifts are used in computing gifts for preceding calendar years. However, the unified rates are used in figuring the tax on these pre-1977 gifts, even though such tax is greater than the amount produced under the old rates. Any U.S. citizen or resident who makes a gift to anyone other than his spouse that is not excluded under the $10,000 present interest exclusion must file Form 709. Simplified Form 709-A may be used by a married couple who elects gift-splitting for gifts that are nontaxable because they are covered by the annual exclusion. This short form is available only for present-interest gifts to third parties that do not exceed $20,000.

If a donor fails to pay any gift tax due, the law provides that the donee is personally liable for the donor's gift tax. The donee is not liable for filing the return.

The use of the unified credit to offset a gift tax liability is not an assessment or payment of tax for purposes of Section 2504(c). Thus, if no tax is paid, the statute of limitations does not start to run, so any valuation issues remain open indefinitely.

33

GIFT AND
NONGIFT LOANS

For all below-market gift loans and other below-market demand loans, a lender is treated as transferring, and the borrower receiving, the amount of forgone interest on an annual basis. In addition, the lender is treated as receiving from the borrower an equal amount as a payment of interest. Foregone interest is the amount equal to the excess of the amount of interest that would have been payable on the loan for the taxable period if interest had accrued on the loan at the applicable federal rate (AFR) and was payable on the loan allocable to the taxable period.

A gift loan causes both gift tax and income tax consequences for the lender unless one of the exceptions granted by Section 7872(c)(1) or (2) is satisfied. For a gift loan, the lender is deemed as making a taxable gift equal to the amount of forgone interest. The amount of the gift is different for a gift term loan and a gift-demand loan. For a gift-demand loan the taxable gift is equal to the forgone interest computed on a daily basis at the AFR, with the transfer treated as taking place on the last day of the calendar year.

The AFR for gift demand and nongift-demand loans is the federal short-term rate in effect under Section 1274(d) for the period for which the forgone interest is being calculated. For a gift-term loan the forgone interest for gift tax purposes is computed on the day the loan is made and is the difference between the amount of the loan over the present value of all required loan payments discounted at the AFR, compounded semiannually. For gift tax purposes, the

AFR for gift-term and nongift-term loans is the AFR in effect under Section 1274(d), compounded semiannually based on the loan term.

Since gift-term loans are deemed as demand loans for income tax purposes, the income tax effects are the same for both types of gift loan. Because the borrower is treated as transferring the forgone interest back to the lender, the lender has interest income equal to that amount. The borrower has no taxable income because the transfer from the lender to the borrower is considered a gift. The borrower does, however, have an interest deduction. The borrower comes out ahead because he gets a deduction without having to make any cash outlay. The lender loses in the transfer because he not only is subject to the gift tax, but also has to recognize income that he has not and will never receive.

Nongift loans, in some situations, produce more favorable tax consequences for the lender than do gift loans. Although the lender must report income equal to the forgone interest, if the nongift-demand loan can be classified as a compensation-related loan (the borrower is an employee of the lender or there is an independent-contractor relationship), a deduction can be taken in that year equal to the interest received. The borrower has taxable income in the amount of the forgone interest, but also has a corresponding deduction for the imputed interest. Thus, the transaction for both borrower and lender can result in a "wash" for income tax purposes.

If the borrower is a shareholder, the transfer is classified as a dividend, and no deduction is allowed to the corporation. Thus, the corporation would have taxable income with no offset. The shareholder could still have a wash transaction if the interest deduction were allowed as an itemized deduction or if it fell within the limits of the investment-interest deduction.

For a nongift-term loan the timing of the taxable investment income and interest deduction is different from that of the demand loan. However, the timing is the same for both gift and income tax purposes. For all nongift-term loans the lender is treated as transferring to the borrower, and the borrower is treated as receiving from the lender, cash equal to the excess of the amount of the loan over the present value of both principal and interest payments due under the loan. The transfer is treated as occurring on the date the loan was made. In addition, the excess of the amount of the loan over the present value of the payments due is treated as original issue discount. Consequently, the borrower is treated as paying, and the lender is treated as receiving, interest at a constant rate over the life of the loan.

The current law essentially eliminates the use of below-market loans as an estate planning tool. There are, however, some escapes from the application of these rules, provided by the *de minimis* exception and special rules for gift loans.

For income tax purposes, no amount is treated as transferred by the lender to the borrower, or retransferred by the borrower to the lender, for any day during which the aggregate amount of outstanding loans does not exceed $10,000. This calculation includes the aggregate amount of all loans between the lender and borrower, regardless of interest rates. For example, if the lender makes one loan for $10,000 to the borrower at a below-market rate of interest and another $10,000 loan at the applicable federal rate, the exception would not apply. Also, the exception would not apply if the borrower uses the money to purchase or carry income-producing assets.

In the case of gift loans between two individuals where the aggregate amount of the outstanding loans does not exceed $100,000, the amount of interest deemed to be retransferred to the lender will be the lesser of (1) the imputed interest on the loan, or (2) the borrower's total net investment income. In addition, if the borrower's total net investment income does not exceed $1000 and the $100,000 test is met, then the retransferred amount is considered to be zero.

Net investment income is the excess of investment income, as defined in Section 163(d), over investment expense. However, this section does *not* apply if one of the principal purposes of the loan is tax-avoidance. It should also be noted that gift tax consequences may still apply. In order to prevent abuse of the rules by deferral or distortion of investment income, deferred-payment obligations (market-discount bonds, short-term obligations, U.S. savings bonds, annuities, etc.) are treated as interest income in computing net investment interest.

This $100,000 exception may prove useful where a taxpayer wishes to make a loan to persons who have little investment income and do not invest the proceeds of the loan (i.e., a college student who purchases a duplex while attending college).

The next key begins a discussion of the trust vehicle, which is about six centuries old. Trusts are important estate-planning devices.

34

PLANNING AND CREATING TRUSTS

The term *trust* is used by courts and lawyers in a variety of senses. Often it is used to include other fiduciary relationships such as bailments, executorships, guardianships, and agencies. However, in a narrower sense, the term is applied to a particular kind of fiduciary relationship that began in England when the courts of law and courts of equity in that country were separated. In this book, the term trust is applied only to trusts in this narrower sense.

Because of the way in which U.S. laws are structured, a definition of any legal concept cannot properly be used as though it were a major premise so that rules governing conduct can be deduced from it. Since there is not one exact or perfect definition of the term trust, this key will give several definitions in order to acquaint the reader with the legal concept.

A trust is a fiduciary relationship in which one party holds property, subject to an equitable obligation to keep or use such property for the benefit of another person. In its restatement of the law, the American Law Institute defined a trust as a fiduciary relationship with respect to property, subjecting the person holding title to the property to equitable duties in dealing with the property for the benefit of another person. This relationship arises as a result of a manifestation of an intention to create it. Stated differently, a trust is a relationship between a trustee and a beneficiary with respect to rights in property, where legal ownership is divorced from equitable ownership, and legal title is held by the trustee exclusively for the benefit of the beneficiary because of the latter's equitable interest. At least one court has defined a trust as a property right held by one party for the use of another.

These definitions of the term trust (and many other definitions) seem concerned with the duty or obligation of the trustee, or with the rights of the beneficiary, rather than with the nature of a trust. The trust in its modern sense is conceived to be the relationship in which the trustee holds the trust property subject to the trust agreement for the benefit of the beneficiaries.

Even though the preceding definitions are not exact or perfect, certain characteristics of a trust may be derived from them. These characteristics are that a trust (1) is a relationship; (2) is a relationship of a fiduciary character; (3) is a relationship with respect to property; (4) involves the existence of equitable duties imposed on the trustee for the benefit of the beneficiaries; and (5) arises as a result of a clear intention to create the relationship. These characteristics give rise to our modern-day trusts.

A trust is a relationship with respect to property held by the trustee. Such property is referred to as the *trust property* and may be defined as the interest in a thing—real or personal, tangible or intangible—that the trustee holds, subject to the rights of another. Aside from the trust property, the relationship usually involves three parties. The settlor (or grantor) creates or intentionally causes the trust to come into existence. The beneficiary is the person entitled to the benefits from the trust property. The third party to the trust is the trustee, who holds the legal title to the trust property for the benefit of the beneficiary.

In a fiduciary relationship, the law demands that one party must have an unusually high standard of ethical or moral conduct with respect to another party of the relationship. In a trust, the trustee is the one required to have such characteristics. Trustees, whether individual or institutional, must represent and act solely in the interest of the beneficiaries; they are not permitted to consider their own personal needs or desires. Owing to the nature of a trust, the trustee is expected to apply more than casual consideration and judgment in dealings with the beneficiary. Being a trustee is serious business.

As far as investing the corpus, or principal amount of a trust, most states have adopted the standard generally referred to as the "prudent man rule." Under this rule a trustee must act as a prudent man (or woman) would be expected to act, avoiding speculative investments and seeking to balance the need to preserve capital and to generate reasonable income. In some states trustees are restricted to buying from a "legal list" of securities.

The settlor, in creating a trust, can state the necessary provisions with respect to the duties and powers of the trustee and the rights of the beneficiaries; unless these provisions are contrary to any local policy or law, they are valid and enforceable. Most of the legal principles and rules governing trusts are applicable only if the settlor does not provide otherwise.

One of the basic purposes of estate planning is to pass the benefits of accumulated wealth from one family member to another in a manner conducive to the best interests of the estate owner and with a minimum reduction of that wealth from taxes. The trust instrument is a valuable tool in estate planning, primarily because it permits considerable flexibility in the disposition and administration of property. The trust device not only saves taxes but also provides the flexibility needed to achieve many of the nontax objectives. Often other factors are just as important as the savings of taxes, such as prudent management of assets and the ability to give someone (the trustee) the right to use discretion as to the amount and timing of income and principal distributions.

(See Keys 42–48.)

35

SUBCHAPTER J TAXATION

Any discussion of estate and trust taxation should begin with Sections 102(a) and 102(b) of the Internal Revenue Code. Section 102(a) provides the general rule that "gross income does not include the value of property acquired by gift, bequest, devise, or inheritance." Section 102(b) indicates that subsection (a) "does not exclude from gross income (1) the income from any property referred to in subsection (a); or (2) where the gifts, bequest, devise, or inheritance is of income from property, the amount of such income." The last sentence in Section 102(b) is the three-way "bridge" between the income tax, federal estate tax, and the fiduciary income tax.

Generally, most people take for granted that any distributions from an estate or trust should be considered "income from property." But this same Code section indicates that "any amount included in the gross income of a beneficiary under Subchapter J shall be treated for purpose of paragraph (2) as a gift, bequest, devise, or inheritance of income from property." The key word is, of course, income. What the Code giveth it taketh away!

Subchapter J fills in this gap between Sections 102(a) and (b). In essence, the distribution rules of Sections 661 and 662 to a great extent neutralize the favorable treatment outlined in Section 102(a). The net result is that most distributions from an estate or trust are treated as taxable income, since they are considered an inheritance (or gift) of income under Section 102(b). There are two major safety valves:

1. Distributions that exceed distributable net income (DNI) are considered to be a tax-free transfer of income under Section 102(a).
2. A specific bequest of an amount of money or property under Section 663(a)(1) is not caught by the distribution rules in Subchapter J (that is, not taxable).

The taxation aspect of an estate or trust involves a number of unique concepts:

1. Fiduciary accounting income (FAI), Section 643(b).
2. Federal gross and net income of the trust, Section 61.
3. Tentative taxable income, Sections 643(a), 61, and 63.
4. Distributable net income (DNI), Section 643(a).
5. Distribution deduction (DD) or Section 651 deduction, Section 651(a) and (b).
6. Taxable income of the trust, Sections 641(b), 642, 61, and 63.
7. Adjusted gross income to the beneficiary, Section 652(a).

The term fiduciary accounting income (FAI) is not defined in the statutes. Instead, Section 643(b) indicates that FAI is to be determined under the terms of the governing instrument and the applicable state statutes. Amounts realized from the sale or disposition of the estate property are allocated generally to the trust (or principal), and day-by-day income items flowing into the trust (or estate) are allocated to fiduciary accounting income (that is, taxable interest, dividends, rent income, tax-exempt interest, and so on). Keep in mind that the trust instrument *or* will may alter the allocation of these income items. The amount designated as FAI is, of course, the amount required to be distributed to beneficiaries, in the case of a simple trust.

Federal interpretation of the gross income of an estate or trust is determined under Section 61, the same income-determination statute for other entities. Next, a figure called tentative taxable income is calculated under Sections 61, 63, and 643(a). As indicated in the prologue to Section 643(a), tentative taxable income is the starting point for calculating *distributable net income.*

36

DISTRIBUTABLE NET INCOME

A unique concept under fiduciary taxation is the term *distributable net income.* Under Section 643(a), tentative taxable income (Key 35) is modified in order to arrive at distributable net income (DNI). These modifications include the following:

1. No reduction of DNI is allowed for the distribution deduction (below).

2. No personal exemption is allowable.

3. Gains from the sale or exchange of capital assets are excluded to the extent that such gains are allocable to corpus.

4. Extraordinary dividends and taxable stock dividends are excluded when dealing with a simple trust.

5. Tax-exempt interest is included in DNI but is reduced by any deductions associated with the tax-exempt interest. Notice that the law mentions tax-exempt interest, but not other tax-free income. For example, a tax-free stock dividend is not included in DNI.

6. Special rules apply to a foreign trust.

Another way of calculating DNI is as follows: start with adjusted taxable income, subtract administration expenses and net long term capital gain allocated to corpus, and add adjusted tax-exempt income.

DNI acts as a limitation to the amount of income that can be taxed to a beneficiary when a distribution is made. The DNI amount also provides a limitation on the distribution deduction (DD) in order to stop tax avoidance through unlimited accumulation of income and use of gifts to charitable remainders.

Think of DNI as a quantitative concept for measuring the amount of income taxable to an estate or trust.

The distribution deduction (DD) is, in most situations, a modified DNI. In order to avoid double taxation to an estate or trust, the statutes provide a deduction for purposes of computing the taxable income of the fiduciary, where income is distributed currently to the beneficiaries. This DD is the smaller of (1) the fiduciary accounting income required to be distributed currently under Section 651(a) or (2) modified DNI under Section 651(b). This "modified DNI" is DNI *less* any nontaxable income included in the DNI. All taxable items on Schedule K-1 of Form 1041 equals the DD item on page 1 of Form 1041. Thus, in general, the income of an estate or trust is taxed only once.

37

AMOUNT TAXABLE TO BENEFICIARIES

The taxable income of an estate or trust is computed in the same manner as in the case of an individual, except as otherwise provided by the law. There are special rules for credits and deductions involving an estate or trust. Thus, both Sections 61 (income) and 63 (deductions) are applicable to fiduciary taxation. Some of the special rules for estates and trusts (rules that do not apply to individual taxpayers) are:

1. A standard deduction is unavailable.

2. Expenditures are not divided into deductions for adjusted gross income and deductions from adjusted gross income.

3. There is no percentage-of-income limitations on charitable contributions.

4. A simple trust is allowed a $300 personal exemption; in general, a complex trust is allowed a $100 personal exemption. If a complex trust is required to distribute income currently (and does distribute all), a complex trust can get a $300 exemption. A $600 personal exemption is available to an estate.

5. A trust or estate is allowed the special distribution deduction (DD) to the extent that distributions are made to the beneficiaries in order to avoid double taxation.

A simple trust is defined as a trust in which all income is required to be distributed currently, does not distribute more than its current income, and has no charitable beneficiaries. All other trusts are complex trusts.

The law indicates that the fiduciary accounting income (FAI) required to be distributed currently by a simple trust is to be included in the gross income of the beneficiaries to whom the income is required to be distributed, whether distributed or not. If FAI exceeds distributable net income (DNI), the amount included in the gross income of each beneficiary is the figure that bears that same ratio of DNI as the amount of FAI required to be distributed to such beneficiary bears to the total amount of FAI required to be distributed to all beneficiaries. In arithmetic terms, this figure is:

$$\frac{\text{Amount of FAI to beneficiary}}{\text{Total FAI}} \times \text{DNI}$$

The tax law indicates that the character of the income in the hands of the beneficiaries is the same as in the hands of the trust (i.e., tax-exempt income for the trust is also tax-exempt income for the beneficiary).

38

DEPRECIATION EXPENSE RESERVE

Whether or not an executor provides for a depreciation expense provision (or depletion) will affect the calculation of the previously mentioned items (i.e., FAI, DNI, etc.). Depreciation is the deduction of the cost of a tangible asset over the asset's estimated useful life. Depletion is the writeoff of a wasting asset, such as an oil or gas field or a coal mine.

Some state laws force an executor to establish a depreciation reserve. If such a reserve is not set up, fiduciary accounting income (FAI) will be higher (to the extent of the depreciation deduction not taken), which in turn affects the amount to be distributed. Since FAI must be distributed in a simple trust situation, the fact that no reserve is established reduces the principal, or corpus, of the trust. In essence, the current beneficiaries receive a distributed part of the corpus. Where a trust is involved with a principal beneficiary and a remainder beneficiary, the corpus that is distributed to the primary beneficiary will, obviously, never be distributed to the secondary beneficiary. Thus, a remainder beneficiary would prefer that a depreciation reserve be established in order to protect the corpus.

If the executor does not establish a depreciation reserve, depreciation expense is allocated among the income beneficiary and the corpus on the same basis as the allocation of FAI.

39

IN-KIND PROPERTY DISTRIBUTIONS

A bequest of a specific sum of money or of specifically described property is not subject to the normal distributable net income (DNI) distribution rules (i.e., treated as a distribution of property and not of income). The distribution must be paid all at once or in not more than three installments.

Suppose a father's will provides for a specific bequest of $36,000 to be paid to his daughter in not more than three installments within 12 months of his death, with the residuary estate to go to his wife. The financial, trust, and taxable net income of the trust for the 12-month period is $30,000. At four-month intervals $12,000 is paid to the daughter for a total of $36,000. Of this, $30,000 came from cash received as income and $6,000 from corpus. No part of this is deductible by the estate for income tax purposes, so that the wife as residuary legatee eventually bears the burden of the estate's income tax liability. Also, the daughter has no taxable income.

Specific bequests of appreciated property can be advantageous because the beneficiary receives a basis that is equal to the property's fair market value as of the date of the donor's death. Therefore, any unrealized appreciation avoids the income tax forever. Since a gift of appreciated property results in a carryover basis, the unrealized appreciation will be taxed eventually.

In-kind distribution of nonspecific bequest property is treated differently than a specific bequest or gift. At the election of the fiduciary, the beneficiary receives a carryover basis in the hands of the estate/trust or the gain or loss is recognized to the trust or estate. Once made, the election is irrevocable (unless consent is received from the IRS).

Section 643(d)(3) allows the fiduciary to elect to recognize gain or loss on an in-kind distribution. If the fiduciary does not make the election on the tax return for the taxable year in which the distribution was made, no gain or loss is recognized, but the amount deductible by the fiduciary and taken into income by the beneficiary as a distribution of distributable net income (or distribution deduction) is limited to the smaller of the basis or fair market value of the property. The beneficiary then takes a carryover basis.

40

COMPLEX TRUSTS

Although there are different sections in the statutes covering complex trusts, the basic rules applicable to a complex trust are similar to those for simple trusts and estates. Essentially a complex trust does not distribute all of the income to the beneficiaries, and, therefore, the trust itself is taxed on such income.

A tier system is used to allocate DNI. This tier method may be summarized as follows:

- *Tier 1* distribution is the amounts of income and corpus required to be distributed by the terms of the trust agreement.
- *Tier 2* distribution is the other amounts of income or corpus which the trustee distributes to the beneficiaries. These tier 2 distributions come from (1) current income not required to be distributed, (2) accumulated income from prior years, or (3) corpus of the trust.

A tier 1 distribution has priority on distributable net income (DNI). If a tier 1 distribution exceeds DNI, then DNI is allocated to the beneficiaries based upon the following formula:

$$\text{DNI} \ \times \ \frac{\text{FAI required to be distributed}}{\text{Total FAI distributions}}$$

If tier 1 distributions do not use up the total DNI, any remaining DNI is allocated to tier 2 distributions as follows:

$$\text{Remaining DNI} \ \times \ \frac{\text{Your Tier 2 distribution}}{\text{All tier 2 distributions}}$$

An exception to this tier system is the *separate share rule* that is discussed subsequently.

A complicated throwback process applies to complex trusts (but not to simple trusts and estates). These rules are so complex that trustees should seriously avoid accumulating income in a trust. Essentially these rules apply when current distributions exceed DNI (so-called accumulation distribution), there were amount of undistributed net income (UNI) in a prior year(s), and the distribution did not accumulate before the recipient beneficiary is born or turns age 21. If these three conditions are met, the accumulation distribution (AD) is carried back to the UNI year(s). A special tax is calculated that is roughly equivalent to the tax that would have been paid if the UNI had been distributed in the prior year(s).

41

SEPARATE SHARE RULE

The approach of taxing distributions to the extent of distributable net income (DNI) regardless of source is not absolute for the sole purpose of calculating DNI for a complex trust. Where one trust has several beneficiaries, a separate share rule treats each beneficiary as a separate trust. Each beneficiary is treated as having separate and independent interest in the trust as if the beneficiary had his/her own trust. However, the trust document must dictate that the trustee is to maintain separate shares.

For example, the trust instrument for the Fluttie trust states that the trustee is to maintain separate shares. The two beneficiaries, Carl and Velvia, each has a 50% interest in the complex trust. During the current year there is $40,000 of DNI. The trustee distributes $20,000 to Carl, but accumulates $20,000 for Velvia's future benefit. Also, the trustee gives $15,000 of corpus to Carl. Under the normal tier system approach, Carl would be taxed on the $35,000 distribution accumulated for Velvia. Therefore, under the separate share rule in Section 663(c), the trust is treated as two trusts and the $40,000 DNI is divided equally among the two "separate" trusts. Thus, only $20,000 is taxable to Carl.

It is important to keep in mind the fact that the trustee has wide discretionary power in these matters. The courts have ruled this holds true as long as the trustee acts in a manner consistent with the long-term interests of the beneficiaries. Thus, in making distributions, the trustee would consider any tax consequences in addition to the immediate needs of the beneficiaries.

The next series of keys show how trusts can be used to avoid probate, reduce estate taxes, and carry out many business and financial objectives.

42

CHARITABLE TRUSTS AND INSURANCE TRUSTS

Trusts may be classified in many different ways: by purpose, by manner of creation, or by revocable versus irrevocable. There are many purposes for which trusts are formed. In fact, a trust may be created to achieve any desired objective, as long as the objective is not illegal or contrary to any public policy or rule of law. Some of the more common types of trusts, classified as to purpose, include insurance trusts, support trusts, charitable trusts, and marital deduction trusts.

Trusts that are originated in an effort to make one or more gifts to a charitable organization are charitable trusts. The American Law Institute defines charitable purposes as (a) the relief of poverty; (b) the advancement of education; (c) the advancement of religion; (d) the promotion of health; (e) governmental or municipal purposes; and (f) other purposes, the accomplishment of which is beneficial to the community.

The charitable trust is thus used to benefit the general public or some large portion of the general public. In contrast, the private trust has as its objective the furnishing of financial benefits to specific individuals or even corporations.

In practice, charitable trusts generally are of two types. In the first type, the charity is to receive the remainder interest of the trust after some noncharitable beneficiary has received the income from the trust for some period of time (a charitable remainder trust). In the second type of arrangement, the charity receives the income for a period of years, with the remainder returning to the grantor or some other designated beneficiary (a charitable lead trust or a charitable income trust).

Also, consideration should be given to the tax effects of charitable trusts. If the trust is established during the settlor's lifetime, he/she receives an income tax deduction and a reduction in the estate. On the other hand, if the trust is established by a will or as a testamentary transfer, the settlor could receive an estate tax deduction. Thus, careful consideration must be given to the types of transfers that should be made, if an estate planner wants to make a gift to a charitable organization. In general, tax savings can probably be maximized by avoiding testamentary charitable gifts in favor of lifetime charitable gifts.

Life insurance trusts today have become a significant part of estate planning. A person can transfer ownership of a life insurance policy to a trust with a child as a beneficiary. The gift is taxable, but any gift tax incurred on the transfer is minimal. The advantage is that the proceeds of the assigned policy are not included in the transferor's estate (if all incidents of ownership are transferred).

In a great many instances, a trust of life insurance proceeds is merged with a trust of other property. Such an arrangement constitutes the so-called pour-over method of implementing an estate plan. Under this method, the will instructs the executor to collect all of the probate assets and pay all debts, expenses, and taxes. Next, the executor "pours over" all remaining assets into a trust—possibly an insurance trust. The trust, under the direction of a trustee, takes over the function of disposing of the assets in the estate.

Life insurance can be excluded from your estate with an irrevocable life insurance trust. Existing life insurance policies on the life of a grantor may be transferred to a trust, but there's a catch. The grantor must live at least three years to avoid the insurance being pulled into the gross estate under the contemplation-of-death rules. Having the trust purchase new insurance is the best method of funding it to avoid this three-year waiting period. Upon the grantor's death, the insurance proceeds go to the trust, thereby avoiding probate.

An irrevocable life insurance trust may be used in conjunction with a charitable remainder trust (See Key 21). The trust will purchase life insurance on the lives of the charitable remainder trust's income beneficiaries. The heirs of the grantor of the charitable remainder trust are often the beneficiaries of the life insurance trust. On the death of the last income beneficiary, the trust will give the insurance proceeds to the beneficiaries/heirs.

Combining a life insurance trust with a charitable remainder unitrust results in income and estate tax savings, along with an increased cash flow to the grantor. Consult your financial adviser and attorney for more details.

43

SUPPORT TRUSTS

Trusts are especially helpful in planning estates where the beneficiaries are minors, aged, spendthrifts, surviving spouses, or incompetents who may not be capable of properly managing the property. If the grantor's objective is merely to support the beneficiary, a trust may offer certain advantages over an outright transfer of property or funds. One of the main income tax advantages of using a trust is that all the income may pass through the trust to the beneficiary, with the corpus returning to the grantor at the expiration of the trust.

A trust that is designed to provide support for the beneficiary is a support trust. Before March 1, 1986, taxpayers had the option of creating a type of short-term support trust called the Clifford trust. The Tax Reform Act of 1986 stopped this popular income-splitting technique, and a grantor or trustee should avoid making new contributions to an existing Clifford trust, since such actions may turn the old trust into a new trust in the eyes of the IRS. The spousal remainder trust is in the same category.

Although these Clifford trusts are no longer valid, there are other trusts that can be used to accomplish the same objectives, as described in the following Keys.

A support trust could provide for the continued administration of the trust property upon the incompetency or disability of the settlor. For example, the trust could provide for the income and principal of the trust to be given to family members during the incompetency of the settlor. This might avoid the establishment of a guardianship administration and the resulting expenses associated with such a process.

44

MARITAL TRUSTS

The two most widely used methods of securing the marital deduction (Key 23) are an outright bequest to the surviving spouse or the creation of a trust from which the beneficiary is entitled to the lifetime income and has enough control over the corpus to make it includable in his/her gross estate at death. Taking advantage of the marital deduction has two primary advantages. First, management duties are shifted from the surviving spouse to the trustee, who is usually much more proficient at managing the trust property. Second, and perhaps most important, the trust may be set up in such a way that the surviving spouse would have to take positive action to prevent the remainder of the trust from passing to beneficiaries designated by the deceased spouse and creator of the trust.

For instance, the trust could be established so that the surviving spouse is to receive the income for life and have a general power of appointment with respect to the corpus; but if such power is not exercised, the remainder passes to the beneficiaries specified by the settlor. Because of the advantages discussed above and the fact that the marital deduction allows the estate owner to pass an unlimited amount to the surviving spouse tax free, it should be obvious that the marital deduction trust should be given careful consideration by the estate planner.

Frequently two trusts are established: a marital deduction trust and a nonmarital trust. The will instructs the executor to pay the exemption equivalent to a nonmarital trust (a bypass trust or an exemption-equivalent trust) to be held for the benefit of the surviving spouse. At the death of the surviving spouse, the assets in the nonmarital trust are not included in his/her estate. In effect, this exemption equivalent amount (e.g., $600,000) escapes taxation in both spouses' estates. The remaining assets pass either to a marital trust or directly to the surviving spouse, thereby qualifying for the marital deduction. These assets would be taxed, however, when the surviving spouse dies.

Various "sprinkling provisions" can be established to allow the trustee to invade the corpus for the surviving spouse or for the remainder person (often a child). For example, one beneficiary might get a larger amount one year because of a large medical bill. Of course, when the surviving spouse dies, the assets in the nonmarital trust pass tax free to the children.

The next key covers an important trust that may be used with non-traditional relationships—blended families, adoptions, and same-sex relationships. (See also Key 49.)

45

QUALIFIED TERMINABLE INTEREST PROPERTY TRUSTS

A qualified terminable interest property (QTIP) trust may be created in order to obtain an elective marital deduction. A QTIP trust allows a person to provide income to a surviving spouse, upon whose death the assets go to whomever the grantor chooses. The surviving spouse must have an income interest in the assets, and no person other than the surviving spouse may be given a life estate in the property. This type of trust may be appropriate where there has been a second marriage. The decedent may wish to control the eventual disposition of the property (such as to the children of the first marriage), but still give an income interest to a surviving spouse and still obtain a marital deduction.

Once assets are transferred to a QTIP trust, these assets will be taxed at the surviving spouse's death or upon any earlier disposition of the income interest. The surviving spouse's estate is entitled to recover from the person(s) receiving the property any tax attributable to the terminable interest assets. This right of recovery extends to all interest and penalties attributable to the additional estate tax. The QTIP included in the surviving spouse's estate is entitled to a step-up (or step-down) in basis under Section 1014(b)(10).

The QTIP trust can have a Crummey power, as discussed in Key 17. This type of trust is used for families with non-traditional relationships. Patchwork and blended families will find the QTIP trust useful (Key 49).

111

46

LIVING AND TESTAMENTARY TRUSTS

Trusts are classified according to the manner of their creation as either made during the settlor's lifetime (inter vivos) or upon his/her death by a will (testamentary). An inter vivos or living trust is administered by the trustee, not only during the lifetime of the settlor but usually also after his/her death. On the other hand, a testamentary trust takes effect only upon death.

An inter vivos trust may be either revocable or irrevocable. The revocable inter vivos trust is one wherein the settlor reserves the power to terminate the trust at any time during his/her lifetime or to otherwise change its terms. Therefore, the settlor has the ability to completely cancel the trust or has the liberty to change the disposition of either the principal or income or both as circumstances change during his/her lifetime. This revocability makes the property includable in his/her estate because of the retained power.

An irrevocable trust is just what the word irrevocable means. Once it is created, the trust agreement cannot be revoked and usually cannot be changed or modified. This restriction means that no beneficiaries may be added.

There are a number of advantages of a living trust during the settlor's lifetime:

1. It is an easy way to have one's investments managed by a financial expert, to the extent desired.

2. It is a simple, expeditious, and inexpensive

way of providing for the payment of bills for one's care if one becomes sick or incapacitated, thereby avoiding the need for a conservator or guardian of the estate.

3. It gives a settlor and his/her family the opportunity to get acquainted with the trustee. If they are dissatisfied with the way the trustee operates, they can replace him/her.

4. It serves as a good means of describing and segregating property according to its nature, the title to it, and the disposition to be made of it in accordance with sound estate planning practices.

5. It is valid in every state, and there are no adverse lifetime income tax consequences.

Some of the advantages of a living trust after the settlor's death include the following:

1. The trust assets do not become part of the decedent's probate estate and are not included in figuring the executor's commission or the attorney's fees.

2. Succeeding beneficiaries can receive trust income and principal immediately after the settlor's death unless tax considerations or the need to obtain releases cause delays.

3. A living trust has elements of privacy and confidentiality not afforded by a will, because the public does not have access to the trust document or trust assets as it does to the probate and court records.

4. The settlor, no matter where he/she lives, can ordinarily choose the state law that governs the trust (in most cases by choosing an attorney in that state). A will must be probated in the state and county of domicile.

5. It is difficult for disgruntled heirs to attack.

47

REVOCABLE
VERSUS
IRREVOCABLE
TRUSTS

People today are unduly tax conscious. Too often the only factor that they consider is whether or not there will be a tax savings and, if so, how much it will be. However, in estate planning of revocable and irrevocable trusts, the nontax considerations can be more important than the tax considerations. The characteristic (revocable versus irrevocable) is very important to the estate planner.

Generally, the irrevocable inter vivos trust is a vehicle for federal tax savings, while the revocable inter vivos trust is more suited for nontax objectives. The choice depends on the settlor's decision—either to transfer the property away forever (irrevocable) or to retain the right to get it back at a later date if circumstances should change (revocable).

The value of the revocable trust is appreciated only when one realizes that it is not permanently binding like an irrevocable *inter vivos* trust but is, in effect, a will. For the purposes of this chapter, a revocable *inter vivos* trust is defined as a trust created during the settlor's lifetime that the settlor alone has the power to revoke.

The basic distinction between a revocable trust and a will is that the former effects a present transfer of property rights subject to "divestment" by exercise of the power of revocation. The will, of course, creates only expectations. The fundamental advantage of wills seems to be that they enable people to determine who shall succeed to their property after their death without requiring them to part with it during their life. Their main disadvantage is that the testator's freedom of disposition is often restricted. However, it is well settled that one has much greater freedom of alienation *inter vivos* than one has freedom of testamentary disposition. Because the revocable *inter vivos* trust effects a present transfer of property rights, it should not be subject to the restrictions on testamentary dispositions. However, because the trust is revocable, the settlor does not run the risk of being unable to recall the property once transferred. There are also advantages to be considered after the death of the settlor.

A revocable *inter vivos* trust that continues after the settlor's death provides for an uninterrupted management arrangement. During the time of existence of the trust prior to death, the settlor has the opportunity to observe the management ability of the trustee and thus be assured that his directions will be followed.

Probate assets of a decedent are more or less in a suspended state until the executor can satisfy the claims of creditors and death tax obligations. The potential personal liability of the executor naturally defers the availability of the use of the estate assets by the beneficiaries until such liability is eliminated.

Also, probate property and its destination are revealed in a decedent's will, and the amount and nature are generally a matter of public record. Decedents may desire to keep their financial records and methods of caring for their families from becoming a part of such record, and to a considerable degree, this may be accomplished by an arrangement that avoids probate, which is usually a trust-property arrangement. However, the items in the gross estate (probate and nonprobate) have to be disclosed in the federal estate tax return. Also, the instrument creating a revocable *inter vivos* trust will be filed with the return. However, the return and accompanying papers are not open to public scrutiny as are probate records. Various state laws may impose on the freedom of a property holder to decide who will be beneficiaries of his/her estate. To the extent that these restrictions apply only to probate property, they can be minimized by avoiding probate. To the extent that they are not limited to probate property, they may be avoided by placing the property under the jurisdiction of a more favorable state. Such a state may be selected by a property holder to establish a revocable *inter vivos* trust with the intention that its law control the trust, provided the trustee and the property are located there. (For a living trust, any state may be chosen.)

It has already been pointed out that the principal advantage of an irrevocable *inter vivos* trust is the saving of federal income and estate taxes. The major disadvantage of such a trust is that it results in the settlor's losing control of the property. Once made, the settlor of an irrevocable *inter vivos* trust can no longer change the terms of the trust to take into account any changed circumstances.

There may be instances when an individual would transfer property to an irrevocable *inter vivos* trust where the tax considerations are secondary. Suppose a man has accumulated an estate adequate enough to provide what he desires for his family, and he realizes that he is reaching an age at which he might not be able to trust himself to make good business decisions. If he makes the trust revocable, he might unwisely revoke the trust, but if it is irrevocable, he has protected himself against this possibility.

Usually, however, when people decide to create an *inter vivos* trust other than a revocable one, they desire to accomplish the two following tax results:

1. The income from the trust will be removed from their taxable income.

2. The appreciation value that occurs after the transfer of the trust property will be removed from their gross estate.

The cost of accomplishing these results is mainly

that the unified tax credit must be used, or, if the trust property is sufficiently large, the payment of a federal transfer tax must be made early. Considering other economic factors related to a reduction in one's wealth, a gift can still be a sound device for estate planning.

Property owners, by making outright gifts during their lifetime, shift the income tax liability from themselves to the people to whom they make the gift. Thus, if they make an irrevocable gift in trust, they may, according to the terms of the trust, shift the income tax liability to the trust or to the beneficiary. If the income is not distributed or is not distributable, it is taxable to the trust. If it is distributed or distributable, ordinarily it is taxable to the beneficiary. But, although the trust is irrevocable, the property owners may have reserved the right to leave themselves substantially the owners of the property, in which case the income would be taxable to them. See Key 48.

48

GRANTOR TRUSTS

A trust under which the grantor retains the right to the income for life, with the remainder going to someone else (but which cannot be revoked), creates a situation that reduces the gross estate only by the amount of the gift tax paid (if any). The grantor is taxable on the income from such a trust because he/she has the right to receive it, and the value of the principal of such a trust is includable in gross estate for federal estate tax purposes. Thus, there is no major tax advantage to be gained by using such a trust.

A grantor who retains the powers of dominion and control over trust property and income is considered to be the substantial owner of that property and is taxable on its income, rather than the trust and its beneficiaries. A typical power would be the right to revoke the trust. Such a trust is called a "grantor trust." The grantor need not actually receive any income in order to be taxed on it. If the grantor or some nonadverse party possesses a prohibited power over the trust's corpus or income, the grantor is taxed on the trust's income. An adverse party is anyone with a substantial beneficial interest who would be adversely affected by the exercise or nonexercise of a power. However, very broad powers can be given to an independent trustee, such as a bank.

A Mallinckrodt trust is an extension of the grantor trust rules. A person other than the grantor can be treated as the owner of any portion of a trust where (1) the person has a power exercisable solely by himself to vest the corpus or income therefrom in himself, or (2) such person has previously partially released or otherwise modified such a power but after the release or modification still retains other powers prohibited to a grantor.

If the trustees or cotrustees have the power to apply income to the support of any individual whom they are legally obligated to support, then they are taxed upon such income but not on any additional sum. This exception to the general applicability of the Mallinckrodt principle is a technical one. The power to use money to support dependents must be possessed by people in their capacity as trustee or cotrustee.

For example, suppose G creates a trust and names a local bank as sole trustee, but she gives her married son the power to appoint the income for the support and maintenance of his minor children. The son is taxable on all the income whether or not used for the support of his children. Suppose the son is a cotrustee with the bank and only in that capacity has the power to appoint the income. Now he is taxable only on the money actually used for the support of his children.

Estate and gift tax benefits may result from a grantor lead trust. A grantor lead trust occurs when the income from property is paid to a grantor for a period of years and the remainder accrues to a younger-generation beneficiary, such as a child. Although the grantor retains the income interest, there is a complete gift as to the remainder. As long as the grantor does not die during the income term, any subsequent appreciation in the property goes to the younger-generation beneficiary free of estate and gift taxes. Where the grantor dies during the income term, Section 2036 would pull the property into the grantor's estate. Thus, the grantor should be young enough to be likely to outlive the income term.

49

NON-TRADITIONAL RELATIONSHIPS

Not all families and friends fall within the traditional relationships. Every 27 seconds or so, someone in the United States gets divorced. The United States has the highest divorce rate in the world—almost twice as high as many other affluent countries. Across our nation are many patchwork families, and there are nearly 2 million couples living together.

Some non-traditional relationships include

- children of former marriages
- adoptions
- co-habitation
- same-sex relationships
- communal living

A valid will is crucial for these situations because most state laws assume that family members—and not friends—are the natural beneficiaries of one's assets.

Many of the usual planning strategies may be used by these individuals, such as lifetime gifts, asset freezes for an interest in a business, sale of a remainder interest, premarital agreement, or a charitable gift of a remainder interest in property. However, the unavailability of the unlimited marital deduction and lack of the two unified credits allowed to married persons make minimizing the federal estate tax liability more difficult.

After a divorce, wills and trust agreements should be revised to divest the ex-spouse of any interests. Although many state laws automatically divest ex-spouses of any rights, these same laws may not apply to trusts. Further, a person may be reluctant to give all assets outright to a second spouse under a will when there are children from a prior marriage. The natural inclination of the surviving spouse is to favor his or her own children. So how do you protect the children of the first marriage?

With a testamentary trust you may give the second spouse the use of some or all of the assets as a beneficiary, with the assets passing to your children. If the new spouse is young, however, the children may have to wait a long time to inherit your assets, For example, the new Mom may be the same age as Dad's kids and may actually outlive the children. One safety valve is to set aside some of the assets in a trust for the children.

Another safety valve for blended or patchwork families is the qualified terminable interests property in trust. Known as a QTIP trust, your property is left in the trust for the surviving spouse—qualifying for the marital deduction—but the assets pass to whomever you specify when your spouse dies. Again, if the surviving spouse is young, there may be many years of conflict as the children wait for their inheritance (See Key 45). For a younger spouse, you may wish to establish an irrevocable trust for the first set of children, funded with life insurance (See Key 42 and 47).

If you and your spouse disagree about estate planning matters, do not use the same attorney. Do not acquire new property in joint tenancy if you wish the assets to go to your children, because joint tenancy assets go to the survivor. Finally, you will need a premarital agreement in a second marriage if you wish to leave all of your property to your children. A surviving spouse has an elective right to one-third of your property in common law states and one-half of your assets in community property states.

50

GENERATION SKIPPING

Estate owners often wish to avoid having to pay estate taxes on successive life estates. Many times the estate owner will be satisfied to skip the tax at the death of the primary beneficiary. This can be accomplished by the use of a trust. The estate owner simply leaves the estate in trust, with the income going to his/her spouse for life and the remainder to the children upon the death of the remaining spouse. There is no estate tax on the property in which the survivor merely held a life interest.

The generation-skipping transfer (GST) tax is imposed whenever there is a transfer to a person who is more than one generation below that of the transferor. This GST tax is imposed at the flat maximum estate tax-rate, which is 50% for those persons dying after 1992 (prior to 1993 the rate was 55%) on all noncharitable transfers that result in the avoidance of the gift or estate taxes in one or more family generation levels below that of the transferor. Sometimes called the Chapter 13 tax, the purpose of the tax is to stop an estate owner from skipping the members of the immediately lower generation in order to deprive the government of the federal estate tax upon the death of the member of such lower generation. This devastating tax is also imposed on gratuitous transfers from trusts where the beneficiaries belong to two or more generations younger than the transferor.

For example, a grandmother establishes a spraying trust for her daughter and granddaughter. When the trustee distributes that income to the granddaughter, the distribution would be a generation-skipping transfer (GST).

Suppose the grandmother makes a $100,000 gift (or leaves a bequest), to her grandson. Not only would the transferred assets be subject to the gift tax (or the federal estate tax), but the transfer would also be subject to the generation-skipping transfer tax. Suppose the gift tax on the $100,000 transfer is $40,000. There would also be a GST tax in 1993 of $30,000 [50% ($100,000–$40,000)].

Suppose the grandmother creates a trust for her daughter, with income to her for life, and upon the daughter's death, the trust assets will go to the daughter's children. Upon the daughter's death, these assets will not be included in her estate, but will be subject to the generation-skipping tax. The tax is computed on a tax-inclusive basis, so if the taxable amount is $100,000 when the daughter dies, the tax would be $50,000 (in 1993) and the granddaughter would receive $50,000.

A generation is determined along family lines. A transferor, his or her spouse, brothers, and sisters are one generation. Their children would be the first younger generation, and their grandchildren would be the second younger generation.

For transfers made outside the family, generations are determined based upon the age of the transferor. Individuals not more than 12½ years younger than the transferor are considered to be a member of the transferor's generation. Individuals more than 12½ years younger and not more than 37½ years younger are considered members of the transferor's children's generation.

The punitive GST is not imposed upon lifetime gifts that are excludible from the gift tax, including the $10,000 per donor per donee exclusion and gifts for medical payments or tuition.

There is also a $1 million lifetime exemption against generation-skipping transfers. For direct skips made before 1990, this exemption was limited to $2 million per grandchild. For a married couple, there is a $2 million exemption. Once an exemption is allocated to transferred property, any further appreciation is also exempt from the GST. Thus, allocate the exemption against property expected to appreciate, and do not allocate the exemption to property expected to depreciate.

Because of the $1 million per transferor exemption, only very wealthy taxpayers need worry about this GST tax.

QUESTIONS AND ANSWERS

Who should have a will?

Essentially everyone with assets or minor children should have a current, valid will. Stories are legion about the disastrous consequences of dying intestate —that is, dying without a will.

Without a will, the state laws specify how the assets are to be distributed. In essence, there will be a will by default. The county or state probate court will appoint an administrator, who may or may not be qualified to manage your estate. In general, most intestate succession laws favor the surviving spouse, children, or grandchildren. Assets may also go to the children of a previous marriage, to distant nephews and nieces, even to enemies.

Parents with minor children should indicate in the will who will care for the children. Unless they do this, the administrator will decide who will be appointed the children's guardian, based on state laws and practices.

Single people living together are especially vulnerable. Most state laws do not recognize a living-together relationship. Certainly the law on intestate succession is especially problematic for homosexuals.

What is a common disaster clause in a will?

A common disaster clause is included in a will to spell out the instructions of the deceased as to the disposition of his/her estate where both deceased and primary beneficiary (most likely the spouse) die in a common disaster. Similar to this clause is the simultaneous death clause, which covers situations in which it is very difficult to determine which person died before the other.

In some wills the common disaster clause directs that the estate shall pass to the trustees if both decedent and spouse die simultaneously. The trustees are directed to divide the estate as instructed in the will upon the death of the surviving spouse.

One reason to include a common disaster clause in a will is to save taxes on the estate. Specifically, it is important for the clause to determine the order of death in order to take advantage of the marital deduction. That is, the surviving spouse in a simultaneous death situation must be the spouse designated as the surviving spouse in the marital deduction provision of the will.

A married couple should put in writing in a custody agreement designating who will rear any children in case of a common disaster.

Whom should I pick as my executor or executrix of my estate?

Any person given serious consideration as a possible executor or executrix should meet several criteria. Qualities of an ideal executor/executrix include experience in the administration of estates; an understanding of the needs and appreciation of the circumstances of the beneficiaries; ability to serve; willingness to serve; knowledge of the nature, value, and extent of your assets; business and investment experience; geographic proximity to beneficiaries and assets of the estate; lack of any conflict of interest; familiarity with your business; integrity and loyalty; competence; and sensitivity.

The next step in the process would entail assembling a list of candidates and devising a rating system to evaluate each candidate. The candidates chosen will most likely to be close friends or family members.

Using the 12 qualities listed above, construct a chart listing all candidates and assign a number rating for each category. A rating scale of 1 through 10 with the higher numbers indicating perceived strengths in each category, would be most suitable for ranking purposes. Assign a multiplier factor of 1.5 to the sensitivity category, since this quality has been found to be more important than the others. A person sensitive to the needs of your beneficiaries can overcome shortcomings in other areas through the desire to learn more about these areas.)

Sum the individual category ratings and select the candidate with the highest combined rating. In addition, designate the two next-ranking candidates as the back-up executors should the primary executor die or be incapacitated.

Can disclaimers be used for estate planning?

A disclaimer allows an individual to postpone decisions that are based upon asset values and estate composition until such values are fixed at death. In essence, a disclaimer or renunciation is an unequivocal refusal to accept an interest or power in property for which a person is otherwise entitled by will, gift, or operation of law. Quite often the disclaimed property is passed to another person.

In order to be qualified, a disclaimer must be an irrevocable and unqualified refusal by a person to accept an interest in property. Also, the disclaimer must be in writing and must be received by the transferor within a specified time. As a result of such refusal, the interest passes without any direction on the part of the person making the disclaimer and passes either to the spouse of the decedent or to another person.

For example, a specific bequest to a charity coupled with a disclaimer in favor of a charity can be a valuable provision in a will. The point here is that if the estate tax rate is less than the income tax rate of an heir, a greater benefit would occur if the heir made the charitable contribution. Further, in a small estate the deduction is wasted on the estate tax return because the estate is less than the exemption equivalent.

What is a prenuptial agreement?

It is simply an agreement or contract that two prospective marriage partners enter into prior to taking their marriage vows. The primary purpose in having such an agreement is to prespecify (which usually means limit) the property rights each prospective spouse would acquire without such an agreement.

The primary concern of such agreements is the distribution rights following the end of a marriage owing to death or divorce. Prenuptial agreements are popular primarily because of the growing divorce rates and the increasing occurrence of remarriages.

The judiciary among the 50 states have not been consistent in their application of prenuptial contracts. However, there are similar standards employed by all states. For instance, the courts disallow those contracts that act to promote or foster divorces. Also, any provision regarding sexual relations will nullify the contract, as well as provisions that try to reduce or eliminate future child-support payments.

In upholding such agreements, the courts generally seek to have demonstrated to them that each party had sufficient knowledge of the other's property, that both had the advice of counsel prior to signing, that the agreement was committed to writing, and that a sense of fair play was provided to both parties. Also, the contract must comply with a state's statute of frauds in regards to its writing, consideration given by both parties, and its execution.

In sum, the states have been fairly consistent in upholding prenuptial agreements following the death of one marriage partner, provided that both parties appear to have been treated fairly.

Under the Retirement Equity Act of 1984, clauses that seek to waive rights in pension assets are generally nullified in prenuptial agreements. However, promises to give up such rights can be written into the contract under specific circumstances. Such waivers could be treated as a taxable gift dependent upon the consideration given.

Do states have death taxes?

Every state has some form of death tax. These state death taxes fall into one of three general patterns: gap-tax states, estate tax states, and inheritance tax states.

The federal government allows some revenue sharing with states in the form of a credit against the federal estate tax. The amount of the credit is determined from tables based upon the size of the estate. A gap-tax state simply collects the amount of this credit against the federal tax. Thus, these gap states receive death tax revenues that would automatically go to the federal government. Either way, an estate's tax liability is the same.

Estate tax states have their own tax rates and rules for calculations of the state tax. They may also combine the gap-system approach with their own calculations. In essence, because these states collect money over and above the federal estate tax, they gain more revenue than the gap states.

Some states apply death tax rates against the value of the estate going to particular classes of beneficiaries. These inheritance tax states have different tax rates applying to different kinds of beneficiaries. In general, the closer the blood relationship, the lower the inheritance tax rate.

What is an estate freeze?

An estate freeze is an attempt by a taxpayer to keep the value of an estate at a minimum value (possibly undervalued) by the timely transfer of a business interest in a family enterprise to a family member or members. This interest may be transferred at full value at this freeze point with the transferee(s) (generally the younger generation) able to enjoy any appreciation in value that occurs in the future. However, the transferor (i.e., parent) ordinarily maintains some kind of control in the enterprise and may enjoy a large proportionate share of the income attributable to the enterprise.

The purpose, of course, is to keep estate taxes at a minimum in the estate planning process. The enterprise is transferred rather than retained in the estate, where it would be subject to taxes on the original owner's death. However, the transferor usually retains "substantial interest" in the enterprise, perhaps through voting control, and/or the benefits of the income stream.

This estate freeze ordinarily is accomplished through some type of reorganization of the enterprise. In such a reorganization, the transferor normally transfers all common stock interests (the right to appreciation of the value of the enterprise over time) to a family member. The transferor (i.e., parent) retains preferred stock, which provides voting rights as well as an income stream of preferred dividends.

A new Chapter 14 values interests when they are transferred so that the rights retained, that are not likely to be exercised, are not overvalued in order to reduce the gift taxes. Chapter 14 applies only when the retained interest is an equity interest. A corporate freeze may be too costly because of the second layer of tax. However, without a second layer of tax, a partnership may still be a viable candidate for an estate freeze. A residence GRIT is still viable, and under certain situations, a GRAT and GRUT may be worthwhile.

How do I establish a trust?

This discussion of trust establishment is limited to Totten trusts and private express trusts. The latter is the most common type of trust and is brought into existence by means of a written document known as the trust instrument. The conditions of the trust are set forth by this instrument. The conditions identify the beneficiaries, designate the term of the trust, define the authority of the trustee, and instruct the trustee concerning the distribution of income and corpus during the term of the trust and at its termination.

results in the creation of a Totten trust. This trust is a form of savings account at a bank or savings and loan association. It is created by the deposit of one person in his or her own name of money in trust for another, such as registering the account as "John Doe in trust for Mary Doe."

What are the advantages of a Rabbi trust?

A Rabbi trust is named after the first person to obtain a letter ruling for this form of irrevocable grantor trust. (See, for example, Letter Rulings 8113107 and 8736045.)

The main advantage from the creation of a Rabbi trust is the assurance to employees that their nonqualified benefits will be paid to them by their employer (e.g., in case of a hostile takeover). The only situation in which a Rabbi trust cannot ensure payment of benefits is when the employer reaches insolvency or bankruptcy. In such cases, the trust assets must be available to the employer's general creditors. However, the trust can include a provision to freeze assets within the trust in the event of insolvency or bankruptcy.

The Rabbi trust should be set up so that there are subtrusts to separate accounts for each participant. In addition, such a trust should have sufficient funding to ensure security, should be structured as an irrevocable trust with an independent corporate trustee, and should have a method for recovering excess assets after all benefits have been paid out. If the trust assets are not available to the employer's creditors, the trust is known as a "secular trust." Here, the employee is currently taxed on the employer's contribution to the trust.

What is a marital deduction?

A marital deduction is a deduction applied to the majority of transfers of property between spouses regardless of whether the state in which they reside is a community-property or common-law state. There is both an estate-tax marital deduction and a gift-tax marital deduction.

Several requirements exist for a marital deduction. One basic requirement in order to take a marital deduction is that the couple must be married at the time the gift is made. In addition, the person making the gift must be a citizen or resident of the United States.

Another requirement for the marital deduction states is that the spouse receiving the gift should receive more than a terminable interest—that is, an interest that ends with time or upon the occurrence of an event. Examples of such an interest include patents, life estates, copyrights, and annuities.

How much property may I give away each year without incurring a gift tax?

Section 2503(b) of the Internal Revenue Code states that taxpayers can make present-interest gifts of up to $10,000 to each donee before incurring a gift tax. A married couple can exclude $20,000 of present-interest gifts per year per donee. The number of donees is not limited by the Code. Thus, avoiding gift taxes is a matter of spreading your gifts. You can give away as much property as you wish without incurring a gift tax as long as you limit each gift to $10,000 per donee per year. Also, there is the unified credit of $192,800 or equivalent exemption of $600,000 can be used to avoid the gift tax.

A husband and wife are allowed to give away tax free an astounding amount of property in a ten-year period. For instance, if a family has four children and the spouses agree to split their gifts, a total of $2 million can be transferred without paying any gift tax (using the 1987 unified credit). Each spouse has a $192,800 unified credit and an annual exclusion of $10,000, which is accumulated as shown below:

$20,000 (annual exclusion)

$$\begin{array}{rl} \text{X 4 children} = \ \$ & 80,000 \text{ per} \\ & \underline{\text{X10}} \text{ years} \\ \$ & 800,000 \end{array}$$

$$\begin{array}{ll} \$600,000 \ (1987 \text{ exemption} & \\ \text{equivalent}) \text{ x 2 spouses} = & \underline{\$1,200,000} \\ & \underline{\underline{\$2,000,000}} \end{array}$$

What may be difficult to appreciate is the concept of using the unified credit as soon as possible. Other things being equal, a taxpayer should give away enough assets to use up the unified credit. Think of it as borrowing the unpaid tax from the federal government. Keep in mind that if income-producing property is given away, income can be shifted to a donee in a lower tax bracket.

Are there any advantages of multiple trusts?

After February 1984, two or more trusts are treated as one trust if they have substantially the same grantor(s) and substantially the same beneficiary(ies) and if one of the principal purposes for the existence of multiple trusts is the avoidance of federal income tax. A husband and wife are considered to be one person for the purpose of this provision.

There were several advantages of multiple trusts before March 1984. Each trust was entitled to a $100 exemption, a $30,000 exemption from the alternative minimum tax, and a separate taxation on its own undistributed income. Now under Section 643(e), these trusts are consolidated and have only one exemption and only one run through the tax brackets.

Many multiple trusts created before March 1984 are irrevocable. Because they must be maintained with separate books and records even though their income will be consolidated for tax purposes, they will be an administrative burden for some estates.

What is a reciprocal trust?

A reciprocal-trust, or cross-trust, doctrine is a judicial concept that switches grantors of trusts in order to prevent tax avoidance. Suppose Harriet creates a trust for the benefit of Carl, and Carl also sets up a trust of equal value for Harriet. Under the terms of Harriet's trust, any income is paid to Carl for life, with the remainder to his children. Similarly, the trust created by Carl provides for income to Harriet for life with the remainder to her children. This strategy is not a valid tax-planning technique, even though, technically, neither grantor has retained a life estate. The courts use the reciprocal-trust doctrine in order to switch the grantors of the trusts. All grantors are treated as if they created a trust under which they retain a life interest, and thereby the trust assets are included in their gross estates under Section 2036 as a retained life estate.

In one court decision, however, a decedent and his spouse created two trusts. The spouse was given a special power of appointment over trusts income and the corpus of the trust created by the decedent for her benefit. The spouse's trust for the decedent's benefit did not grant him a power of appointment. Here the

Tax Court held that the reciprocal-trust doctrine did not apply because of the limited difference in the disposition patterns of the two trusts.

The *apocalypse trust* is another type of trust that is meeting opposition from the IRS. Under such an arrangement a taxpayer transfers all assets to a trust and also assigns his/her lifetime services to the trust. For example, a doctor or dentist may transfer his/her place of business to a trust. The beneficiaries are generally the taxpayer's family, with the grantor retaining broad powers over the income and corpus of the trust. The trust collects all of the taxpayer's income and deducts all of the taxpayer's expenses. The purpose of this arrangement is to shift income to taxpayers in lower tax brackets as well as to avoid the estate tax. Four revenue rulings bar the use of these apocalypse trusts.

Are unpaid income taxes deductible on the final estate tax return?

When a person dies, there often will be some unpaid taxes due. Reg. 20.2053-6 (f) provides that such unpaid taxes are deductible on the decedent's estate tax return. If a joint return is filed for the decedent by the surviving spouse, the estate tax deduction is computed as follows:

$$\frac{\text{Decedent's Separate Tax}}{\text{Both Separate Taxes}} \times \text{Joint Return Tax}$$

Sometimes the will provides that only a portion of the residue of the estate shall pass to the surviving spouse. The residue of the estate is the gross estate less debts, administrative expenses, losses, specific bequests, charitable bequests, state death taxes, and the federal estate taxes. Thus, there is a chicken-and-egg problem because in order to determine the amount of the federal and state taxes payable, the marital deduction must be known. But in order to determine the residue amount, the federal and state taxes payable must be known. Which comes first—the residue, the marital deduction, or the residue? IRS Publication 904, *Interrelated Computations for Estate and Gift Taxes* (June, 1982), provides the mathematical approach to solve this dilemma (i.e., simultaneous equations).

Do separate rules apply to a nonresident alien?

Yes. Lifetime transfers are subject to the same rates that apply to a resident, but death transfers are subject to substantially lower progressive rates from 6% to 30%. The unified gift tax credit is not available to a nonresident alien and the estate tax credit is limited to $3,600. Finally, the marital deduction and the gift-splitting election are not available to a nonresident alien.

May trusts be used to shelter my estate from Medicaid providers in case of serious illness or nursing home care?

Certain trusts may be used to render assets legally unavailable to Medicaid providers. Many Medicaid qualifying trusts do not disqualify beneficiaries from receiving Medicaid benefits, however. The Medicaid disqualification period may be as long as 30 months from the date of any transfer of asset to an irrevocable trust. But a properly drafted irrevocable trust may start the running of the disqualification period. For more information about Medicaid, see *Keys to Understanding Social Security Benefits*, published by Barron's.

I am an adopted child. How does that affect my inheritance?

Depending upon your state, the matter of your inheritance is subject to widely varying treatment. Under the Uniform Adoption Act, which has been enacted in at least six states, and followed in other states (e.g., California, Florida, New York), an adoption creates a complete severance from biological roots and a complete assimilation into the new family. There are other states where an adoptee may inherit only from the biological family (and not from the adoptive parents).

May I sell appreciated property in exchange for a series of periodic payments in order to reduce my estate?

The series of payments may be structured in at least four ways: a regular installment note, a self-cancelling installment note (SCIN), a private annuity for a term of years (PATY), or a private annuity. The tax consequences of each approach are different, and you should contact a tax advisor to learn how these four arrows may be used in your planning quiver.

Is there any way for me to maintain control over some assets inside an irrevocable trust?

Trusts called GRITS, GRATS, and GRUTS allow a grantor under limited circumstances to obtain income for a specified period of time and at the same time keep the assets out of the gross estate. A qualified residence GRIT can result in huge savings.

GLOSSARY

Accumulation distribution resulting amount when current distributions exceed distributable net income for a trust or estate.

Adjusted gross estate (AGE) intermediate step in the calculation of certain estate tax concepts. Gross income *less* deductions allowable under Code Sections 2053 and 2054 (expenses, indebtedness, taxes, and losses) result in AGE.

Adjusted taxable gifts any taxable gifts made by an estate in 1977 and later years; not to include gifts made in contemplation of death.

Adverse party anyone with a substantial beneficial interest who would be adversely affected by the exercise or nonexercise of a power, especially with respect to a trust.

Alternate valuation date valuation date six months (*not* 180 days) after the decedent's date of death. For estate tax purposes, the executor may place a value on the estate as of the date of death or on the alternate valuation date, generally choosing the date on which the total value is lower.

Annual exclusion amount of up to $10,000 per donee per year that a donor may exclude from the gift tax.

Annuitant individual entering a contract to set up an annuity.

Asset freeze occurs when the interest of a business is restructured in order for the older owner to receive an interest that has a fixed liquidation value and a preferred income position. Any appreciation in the value of the business is thus shifted to the younger generation and removed from the older owner's estate.

Beneficiary person entitled to the benefits from the trust property.

Blockage discount discount from fair market value for a decedent's block of stock for purposes of determining the valuation of an estate.

Charitable remainder annuity trust trust that is to pay its income beneficiary (or beneficiaries) a specific sum that is not less than 5% of the initial fair market value of all property placed in the trust.

Charitable remainder unitrust trust that is to pay the income beneficiary (or beneficiaries) a fixed percentage that is not less than 5% of the net fair market value of its assets (as valued annually).

Charitable trust trust originated in an effort to make one or more gifts to a charitable organization.

Clifford trust trust created specifically for the retention of a reversionary interest. Formerly useful to parents looking for a way to save money for their children's education, this type of trust was eliminated by the Tax Reform Act of 1986.

Codicil amendment to a will.

Community property property acquired during marriage and recognized in nine states (Arizona, California, Idaho, Louisiana, Nevada, New Mexico, Texas, Washington, and Wisconsin), whereby the law presumes the property to be the product of joint efforts. Thus, in a divorce the couple's total property is divided in half, unless a negotiated settlement is reached, even if most of the assets were earned by one member of the couple.

Compensation-related loan type of nongift demand loan where the borrower is an employee of, or an independent contractor hired by, the lender.

Contingent remainder interest in an estate that does not come into enjoyment and possession unless a certain condition or contingency occurs; or, an interest that may terminate upon the occurrence (or nonoccurrence) of an event in the future.

Corpus term used for the principal of a trust.

Credit for foreign death taxes credit against the

federal estate tax for any inheritance, estate, legacy, or succession tax paid to a foreign country and its political subdivisions on any property that is included in the decedent's gross estate.

Crummey power noncumulative power to invade a trust's corpus on December 31 of each year to the extent of $5,000 or 5% of the corpus (whichever is greater). This power is a general power of appointment only on December 31.

Curtesy *see* Dower.

Date of gift date the donor's dominion and control over the property ceases.

Decedent dead person.

Disclaimer allows a person to postpone decisions that are based upon asset values and estate composition until such values are fixed at death.

Distributable net income (DNI) unique concept under fiduciary taxation, which is the result of deducting administration expenses and net long-term capital gain allocated to the trust's principal amount, or corpus, from adjusted taxable income, and then adding adusted tax-exempt income.

Distribution deduction modified DNI; represents the *smaller* of (1) the fiduciary accounting income required to be distributed currently under Section 651(a) *or* (2) modified DNI under Section 651(b).

Donor person making a gift.

Donee person receiving a gift.

Dower statutory provision in a common-law state that directs a certain portion of the estate (often one third) to the surviving spouse. The term *curtesy* is used if the surviving spouse is the husband.

Estate planning art of designing a program for the effective enjoyment, management, and disposition of property at the minimum possible tax cost.

Estate tax tax imposed on the fair market value of all assets, less liabilities, held by a person at death.

Estate tax payable result of deducting (1) unified credit, (2) state death taxes, (3) gift taxes paid on gifts made before 1977, (4) foreign death taxes, and (5) estate taxes on prior transfers to decedent from the tax before unified credit.

Executor or executrix person designated by will to manage the assets and liabilities of the decedent.

Fair market value price at which an item would be sold at retail. For stocks and bonds this is the mean value between the highest and lowest selling prices on the date of valuation.

Fatal disposition disposition of holding company stock (which is treated as business company stock) or the withdrawal of money or other property from the holding company.

Federal gift tax progressive tax levied upon transfer of gifts from one person to another person.

Fiduciary accounting income includes day-to-day income items flowing into the trust or estate such as taxable interest, dividends, rent income, tax-exempt interest, etc.

Forgone interest amount equal to the excess of (1) the amount of interest that would have been payable on the loan for the taxable period if interest accrued on the loan at the applicable federal rate (AFR) and was payable on the loan.

Future interest reversions, remainders, and other interests or estates, whether vested or contingent, and whether or not supported by a particular interest or estate, which are limited to commence in use, possession, or enjoyment at some future date.

General power of appointment one under which holders have the right to dipose of the property in favor of (1) themselves, (2) their estate, (3) their creditors, or (4) the creditors of their estate.

Generation-skipping tax estate tax on generation-skipping trusts, which is triggered when there is termination of the benefits to the in-between generation or when there is a distribution of trust corpus to the ultimate beneficiary of the trust.

Generation-skipping trust trust through which a person passes property to someone at least two generations younger, with some control or benefits of the property first going to an individual of the in-between generation.

Gift splitting process whereby a husband and wife may combine their annual exclusions and unified credits.

Gift tax excise tax imposed on the transfer of a taxable amount of property during life or upon death.

Grantor lead trust occurs when the income from property is paid to a grantor for a period of years and the remainder accrues to a younger-generation beneficiary.

Grantor trust trust under which the grantor retains the right to the income for life. After the grantor's death the remainder goes to the beneficiary(ies). This type of trust cannot be revoked.

Gross estate total value of all the property, including real or personal, tangible or intangible, owned in whole or in part by the decedent at the time of death to the extent of the value of any interest in such property. *See also* Net estate.

Grossed-up gift result of adding the gift tax paid by the decedent of the estate back to the gift when it is included in the gross estate.

Holographic will will in one's own handwriting.

"I love you" will will tailored to married couples with small estates in which all assets are left to the surviving spouse.

Income in respect of decedent income earned by a decedent prior to his or her death but not yet received (i.e., unpaid salaries, royalties, commissions, interest).

Incomplete gifts gift that does *not* achieve the objective of removing property from the gross estate of the donor. Includes gifts in contemplation of death, transfers with a retained life interest, transfers taking effect at death, and revocable transfers.

Inheritance tax state tax based on the value of property passing to each particular heir. Differs from estate tax in that the degree of kinship of the heir to the decedent generally determines the exempt amounts and tax rates.

Inter vivos term given to a trust created during the lifetime of the decedent.

Intestate having made no will; used to identify a situation in which a person dies without a will.

Irrevocable trust trust agreement that cannot be revoked and usually cannot be changed or modified.

Joint tenancy joint control over the property or interest is only during the lifetime of the tenants. Upon the death of a joint tenant, such interest passes automatically to the surviving joint tenant.

Kiddie tax tax on all unearned income of more than $1,000 received by a child under age 14.

Life insurance trust refers to the use of the trust for the disposition of life insurance proceeds. This type of trust has become a significant part of estate planning.

Lifetime gifts effective vehicle of transfer in estate planning. Gifts eliminate all probate and administration expenses on the property transferred.

Mallinckrodt trust any portion of a trust is considered to be owned by a person other than the grantor if (1) the person has a power exercisable solely by himself to vest the corpus of the trust, or (2) such person retains other power prohibited to a grantor.

Marital deduction deduction available to the surviving spouse of a decedent. Only the net amount of property that passes to the surviving spouse is allowed as a marital deduction. This deduction is also available to arrive at a value for taxable gifts of property given to a spouse.

Marital deduction trust refers to the creation of a trust from which a spouse is entitled to the lifetime income and over which the spouse has enough control to make the corpus includable in his or her gross estate at death.

Net estate *see* Gross estate.

Net investment income excess of investment income over investment expense.

Nonmarital trust   trust that is created for the purpose of avoiding taxation on the exemption equivalent amount (e.g., $600,000).

Nuncupative will   oral will that is generally not held to be valid.

Obligor   party who receives cash or other property from an annuitant in exchange for the unsecured promise to make periodic payments of money to the annuitant for a specific period of time.

Per capita   for each person; requires an equal division of an estate to each person irrespective of relationship to the decedent.

Per stirpes   by family stock; in a trust or similar document, used to indicate that the children of a deceased beneficiary shall receive equal parts of their parent's share of an estate.

Pooled income fund   future interest similar to a charitable remainder trust, except that the donor's irrevocable gifts are commingled with similar contributions in a fund maintained by the organization to which the remainder interest is contributed.

Power of attorney   written instrument by which people appoint an attorney-in-fact to act as their agent and give him/her the authority to act in their behalf.

Pour-over method   method of implementing an estate plan whereby the will instructs the executor to collect all of the probate assets and pay all debts, expenses, and taxes. Next, the executor transfers, or pours over, all remaining assets into a trust.

Prenuptial agreement   contract between prospective spouses in which they outline mutual promises concerning their respective rights after marriage. Increasingly used in second marriages and marriages in later life.

Present interest   unrestricted right to the immediate use, possession, or enjoyment of property or the income from property.

Private annuity   arrangement in which a transferor transfers property to a transferee in exchange for the

transferee's unsecured promise to make periodic payments for the remainder of the transferor's life.

Private trust   trust that has as its objective the furnishing of financial benefits to individuals or corporations.

Probate assets   those assets in an estate that are subject to probate and court disposition and thus become part of public records.

Qualified terminable interest property (QTIP) trust   trust that allows a person to provide income to a surviving spouse, but upon his/her death, the assets go to whomever the grantor (original spouse) chooses.

Reciprocal trust   judicial concept that switches grantors of trusts in order to prevent tax avoidance; also called *cross trust*.

Remainderperson   beneficiary of a trust other than the life beneficiary. This person receives the corpus after the death of the life beneficiary.

Reversionary interest   term used to describe a situation in which the property transferred by the decedent may return to the decedent's estate or may be subject to a power of disposition by the decedent.

Revocable inter vivos trust   trust created during the settlor's lifetime which the settlor alone has the power to revoke and in which the effect of the revocation is to force the return to the corpus to the settlor.

Revocable transfers   term used for property transferred back into a decedent's gross estate.

Separate share rule   rule that treats each beneficiary as a separate trust where one trust has several beneficiaries.

Settlor   person in the trust relationship who creates or intentionally causes the trust to come into existence. Other terms used to designate this person include *donor, trustor,* or *grantor.*

Special power of appointment   power to appoint anyone other than the four parties covered by the relevant general power of appointment.

Special-use valuation   practice of applying the value

of property being used for farming purposes or closely held businesses at an amount lower than its highest and best use.

Spendthrift clause a clause within a trust to protect assets from many sources of liability by giving the trustee the discretion to distribute income and principal (e.g., if needed for health and support).

Sprinkling provision provision that is established to allow the trustee to invade the corpus for the surviving spouse or for the remainderperson.

Step up in basis practice of including appreciated assets in the estate at their fair market value at the date of death or on an alternate valuation date exactly six months later.

Subchapter J portion of the Internal Revenue Code that fills in the gap between Sections 102(a) and (b). Essentially, most distributions from an estate or trust are treated as taxable income.

Support trust trust that is designed to provide support for the beneficiary.

Tax before unified credit result of deducting the amount of gift taxes paid on gifts made after 1976 from the tentative estate tax.

Taxable estate result of subtracting any marital deduction and charitable contributions from the adjusted gross estate.

Tenancy by the entirety *see* Joint tenancy.

Tenancy in common undivided fractional interest in property wherein the owner maintains control over such interest during lifetime and at death.

Tentative estate tax result of applying the unified tax rate table to the amount of the tentative tax base.

Tentative tax base result of adding adjusted taxable gifts to the taxable estate.

Terminable interest interest that will fail with the passage of time or with the occurrence of event or contingency. Such an interest is normally ineligible for the marital deduction.

Testamentary term given to a trust created at the death of the decedent.

Three-part will will in which some assets pass directly to the spouse, some property goes into a bypass trust, and the remaining property passes to a qualified terminable interest property trust.

Trust fiduciary relationship in which one party holds property subject to an equitable obligation to keep or use such property for the benefit of another person.

Trustee person who holds the legal title to the trust property for the benefit of the beneficiary.

Trust property interest in a thing—real or personal, tangible or intangible—that the trustee holds, subject to the rights of another.

Tuition amounts paid to an educational organization that normally maintains a regular faculty and curriculm and normally has a regularly enrolled body of pupils in attendance at the place where its educational activities are regularly carried on.

Two-part will will in which some assets pass directly to the surviving spouse while the remaining assets are deposited in a bypass trust.

Unified credit credit for both the estate tax and the gift tax, which is deducted directly from the gross estate tax to determine the net estate tax payable. The amount of this credit is $192,800. Based on 1993 tax rates, this means that an estate valued at $600,000 passes to the beneficiaries free of federal estate tax.

Uniform Gifts to Minors Act act under which a gift of money may be made by an adult to a minor by depositing it with a bank or savings and loan association in the name of the donor.

Will legal document that serves as a key vehicle of transfer at death. Within the document are specific instructions as to the disposition of the estate and the designated executor (executrix).

INDEX